I0488149

Beyoncé

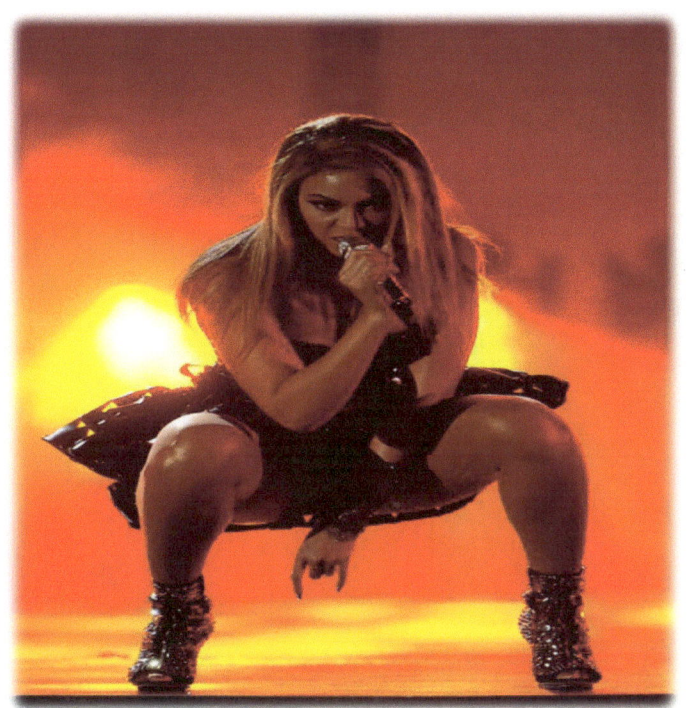

Beyoncé Photo Booklet

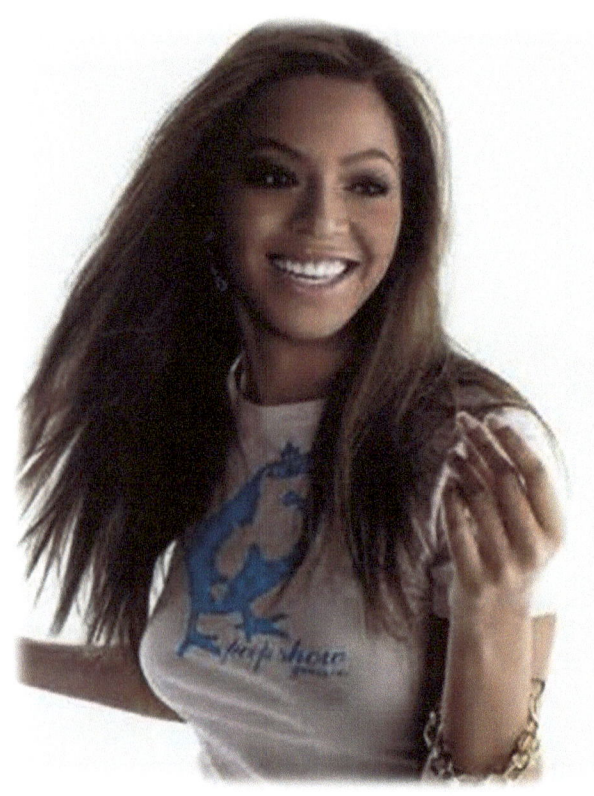

Beyoncé Giselle Knowles-Carter (born September 4, 1981) is an American singer and actress. Born and raised in <u>Houston</u>, <u>Texas</u>, she performed in various singing and dancing competitions as a child, and rose to fame in the late 1990s as lead singer of <u>R&B</u> girl-group <u>Destiny's Child</u>. Managed by her father <u>Mathew Knowles</u>, the group became one of the world's <u>best-selling girl groups</u> of all time. Their hiatus saw the release of Beyoncé's debut album, <u>*Dangerously in Love*</u> (2003), which established her as a solo artist worldwide; it sold 11 million copies, earned five <u>Grammy Awards</u> and featured the <u>*Billboard*</u> <u>Hot 100</u> number-one singles "<u>Crazy in Love</u>" and "<u>Baby Boy</u>".

Beyoncé Photo Booklet

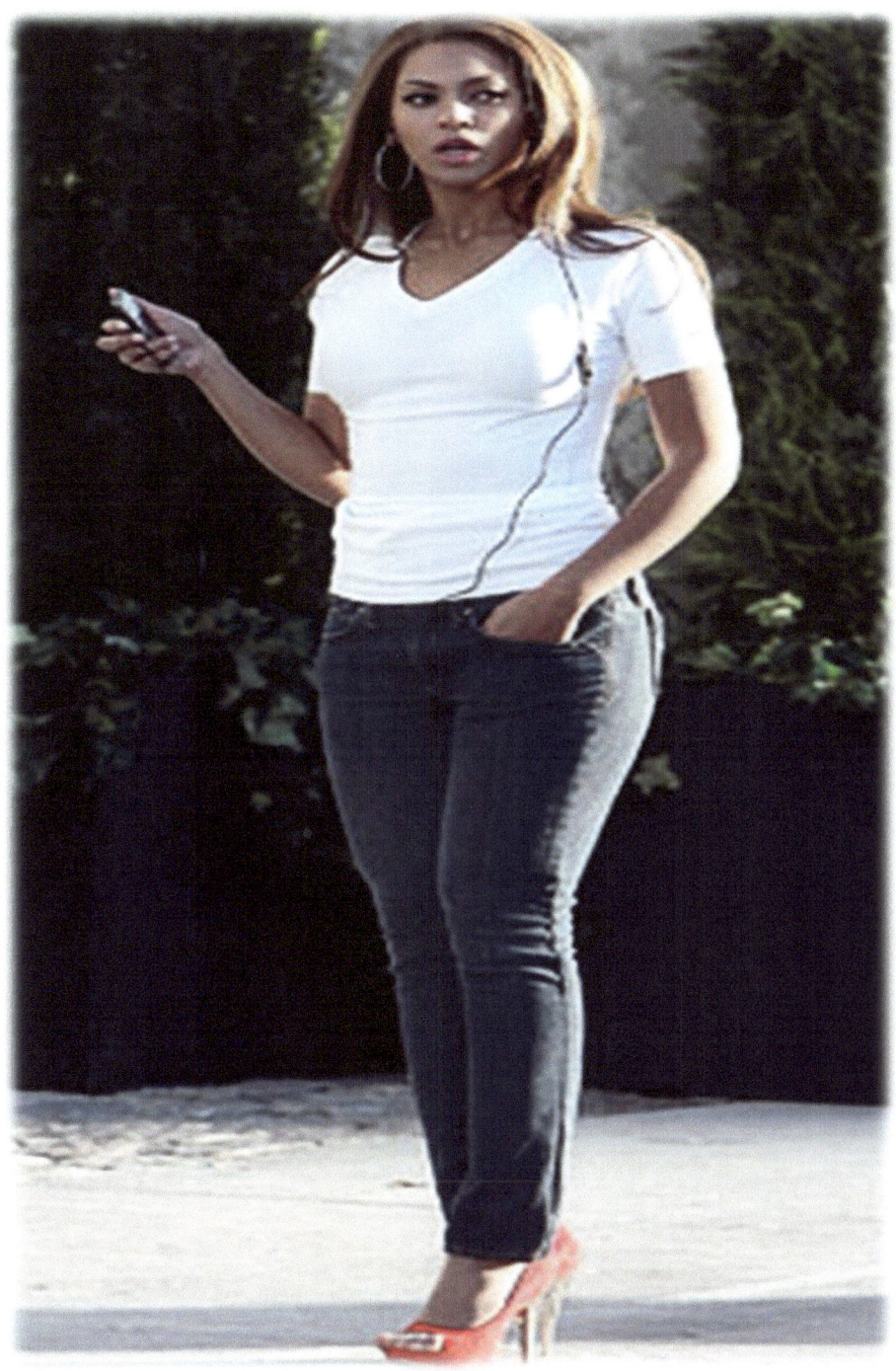

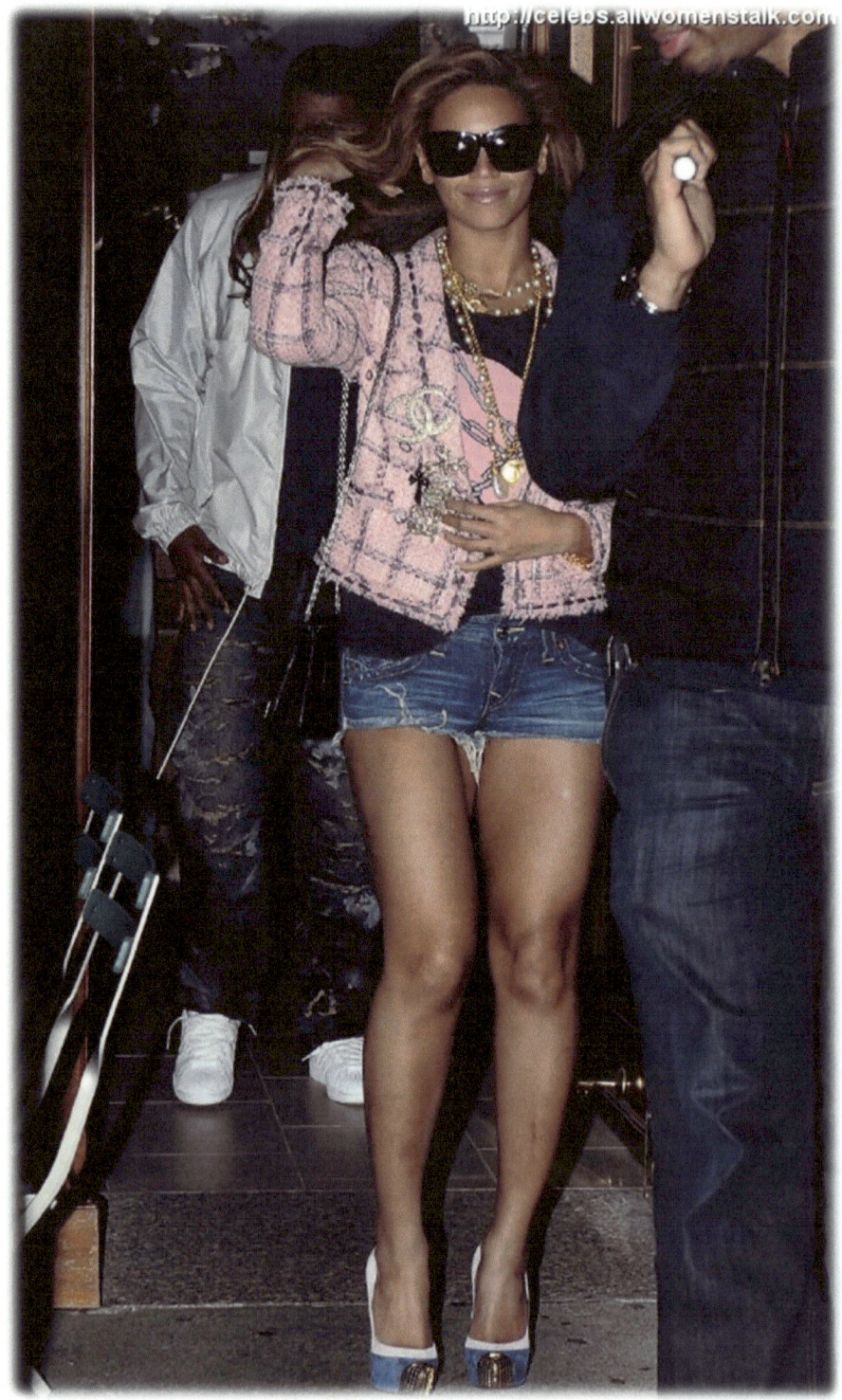

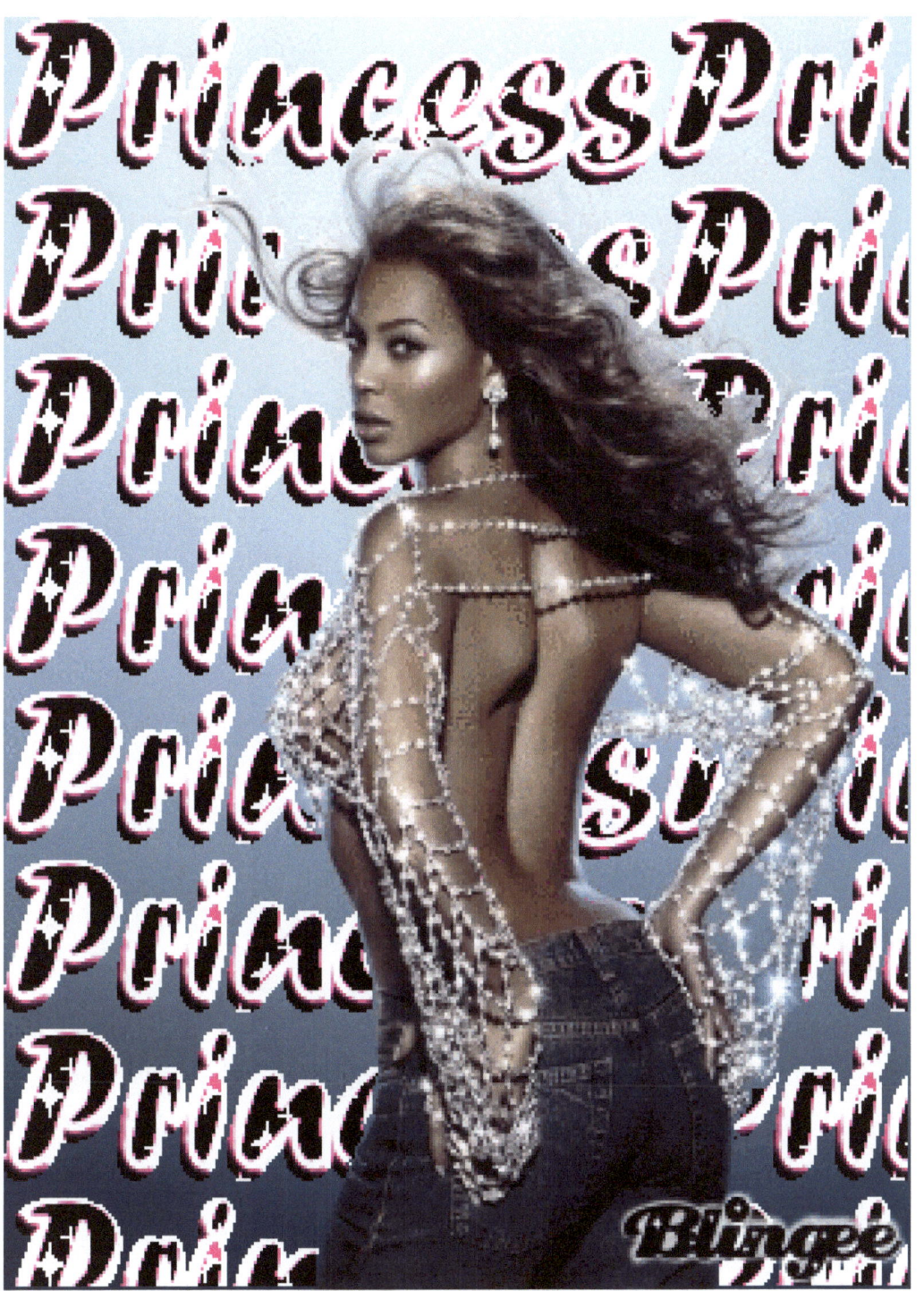

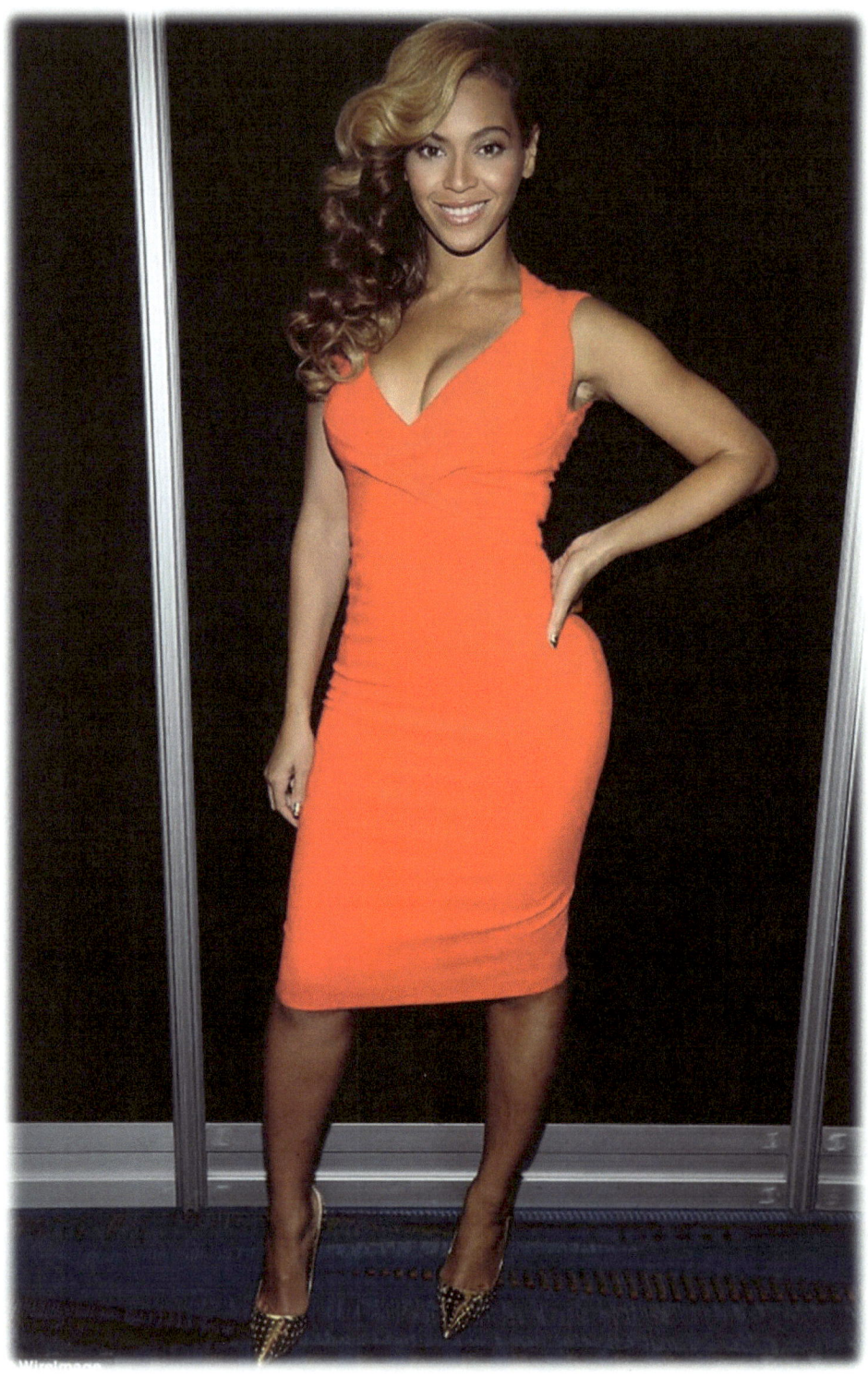

Beyoncé Photo Booklet

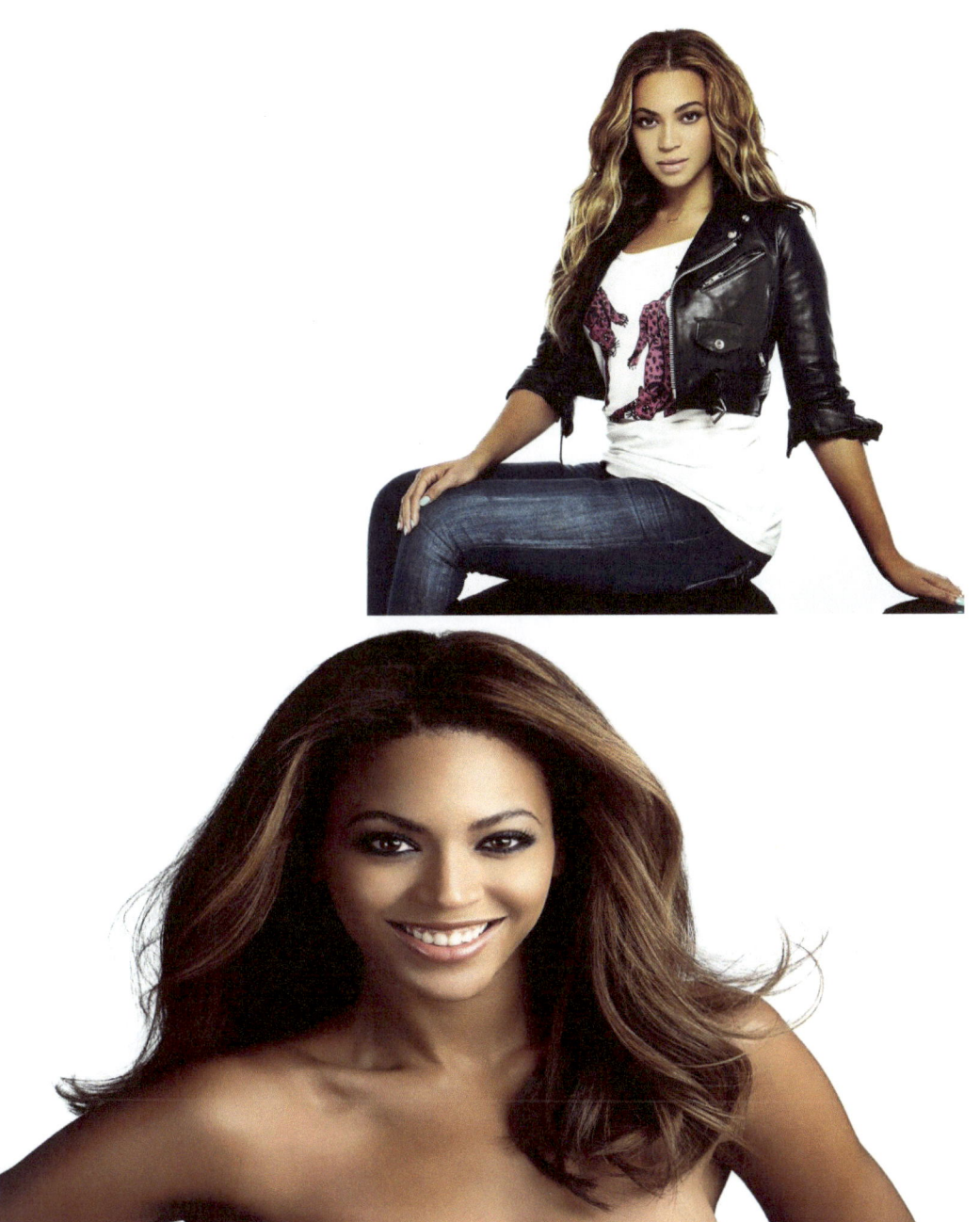

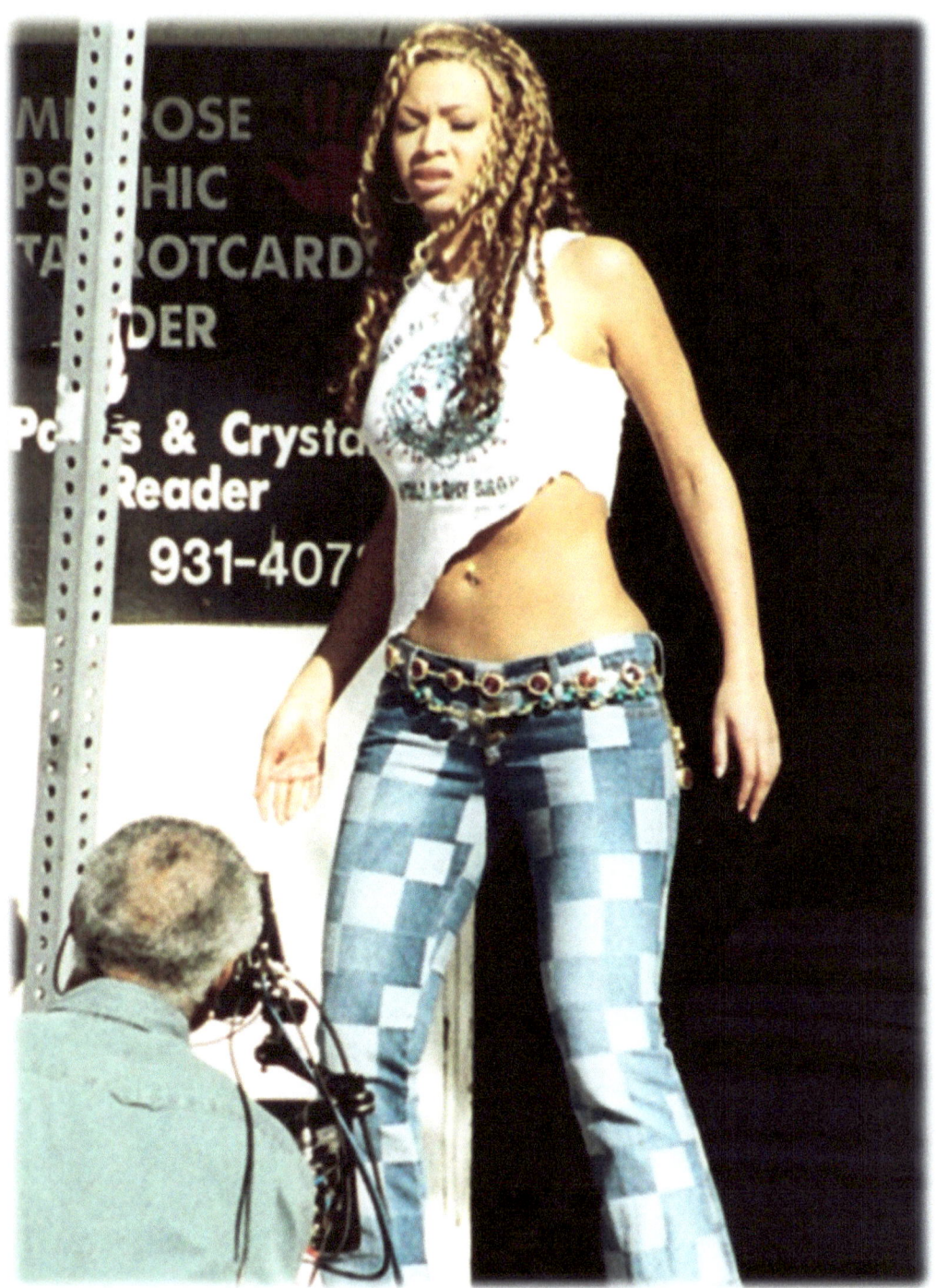

Beyoncé Photo Booklet

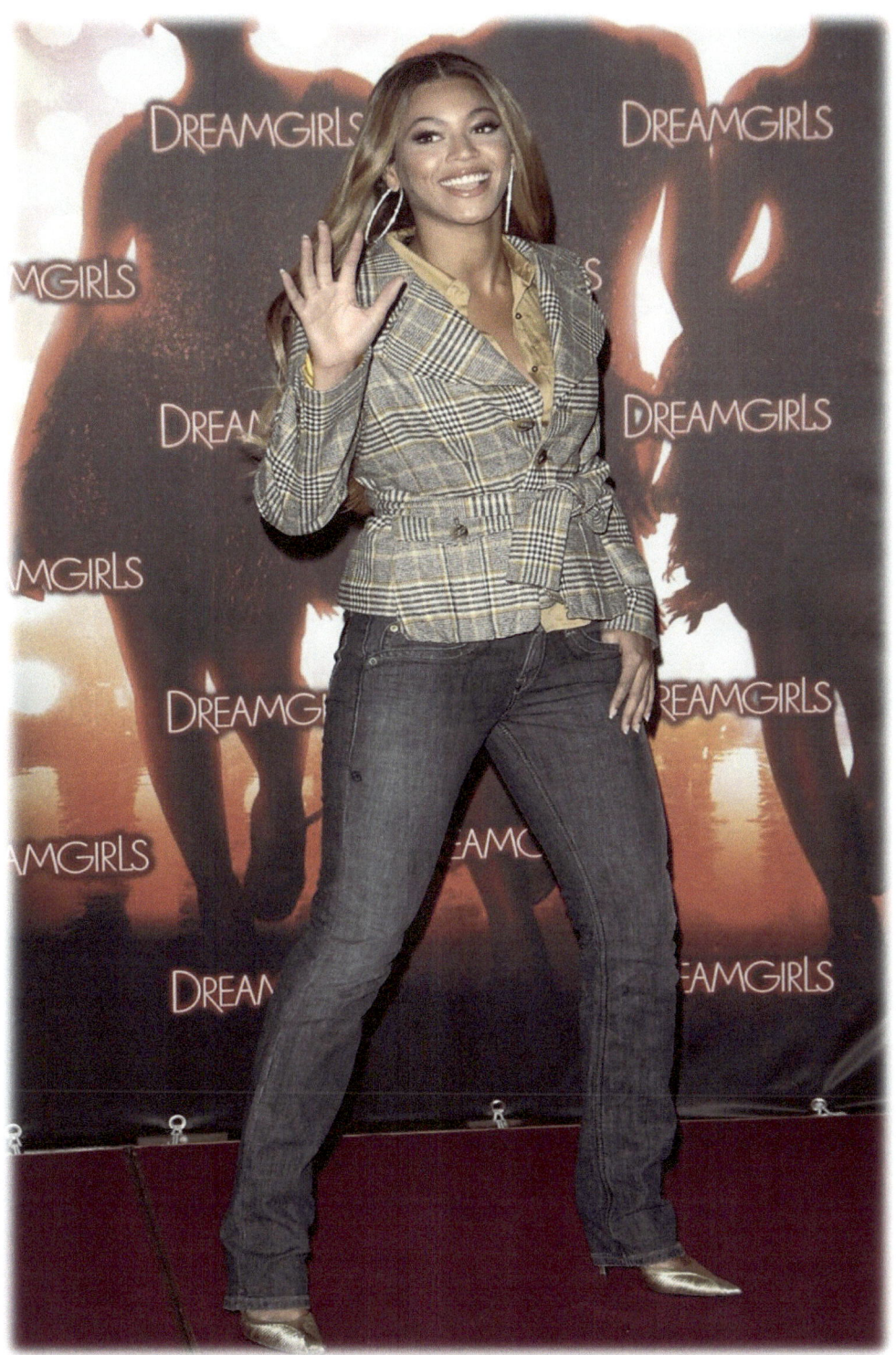

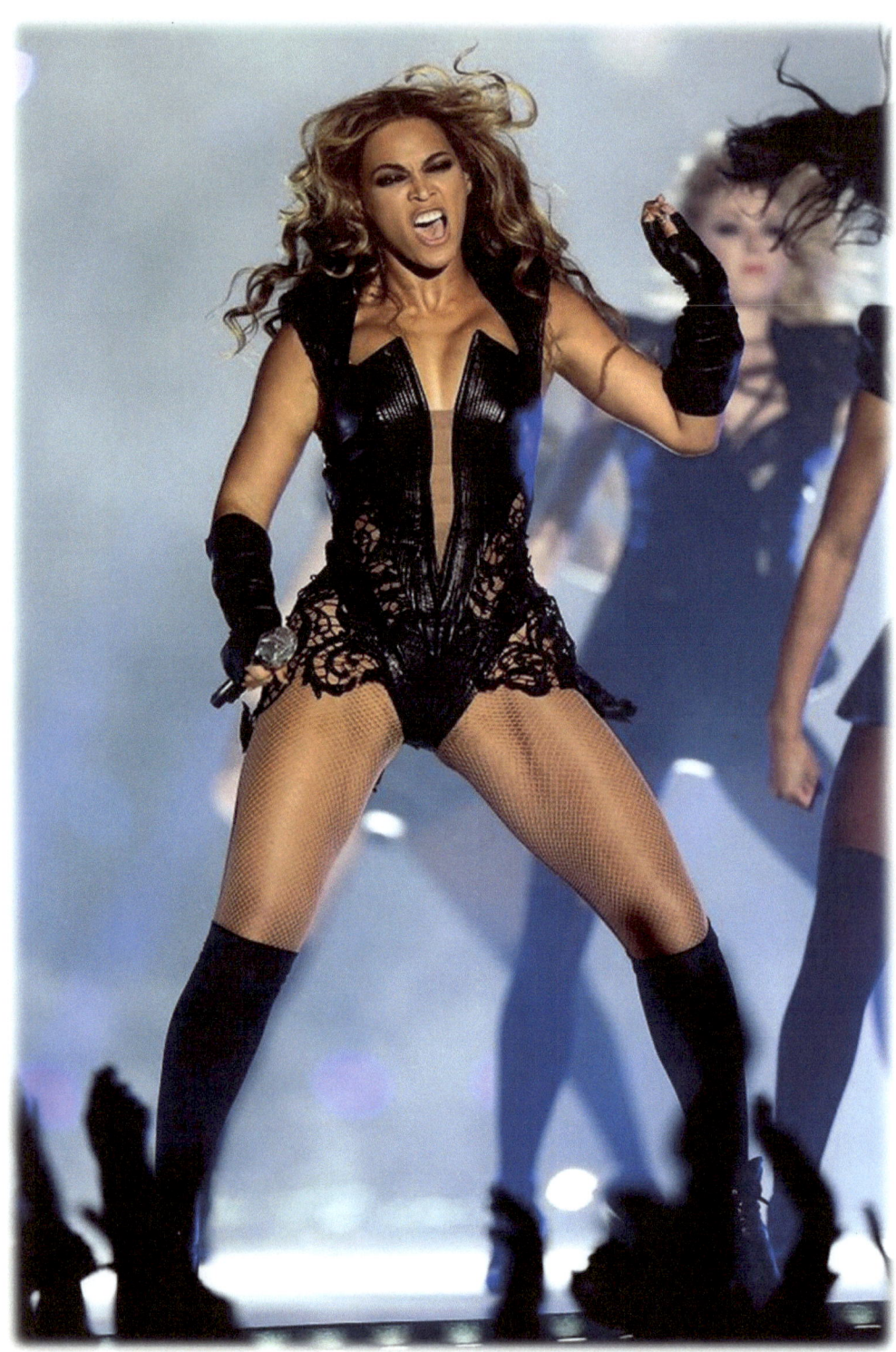

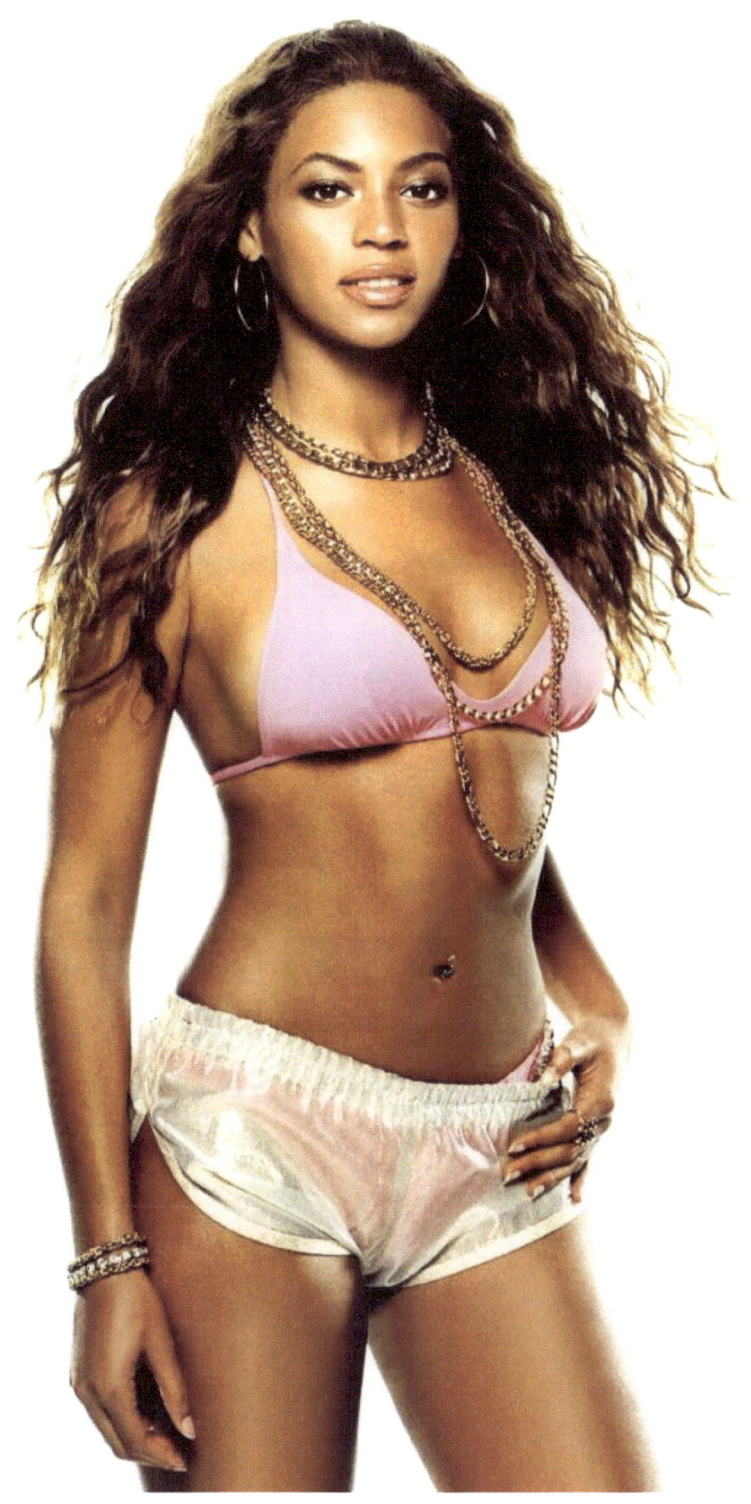

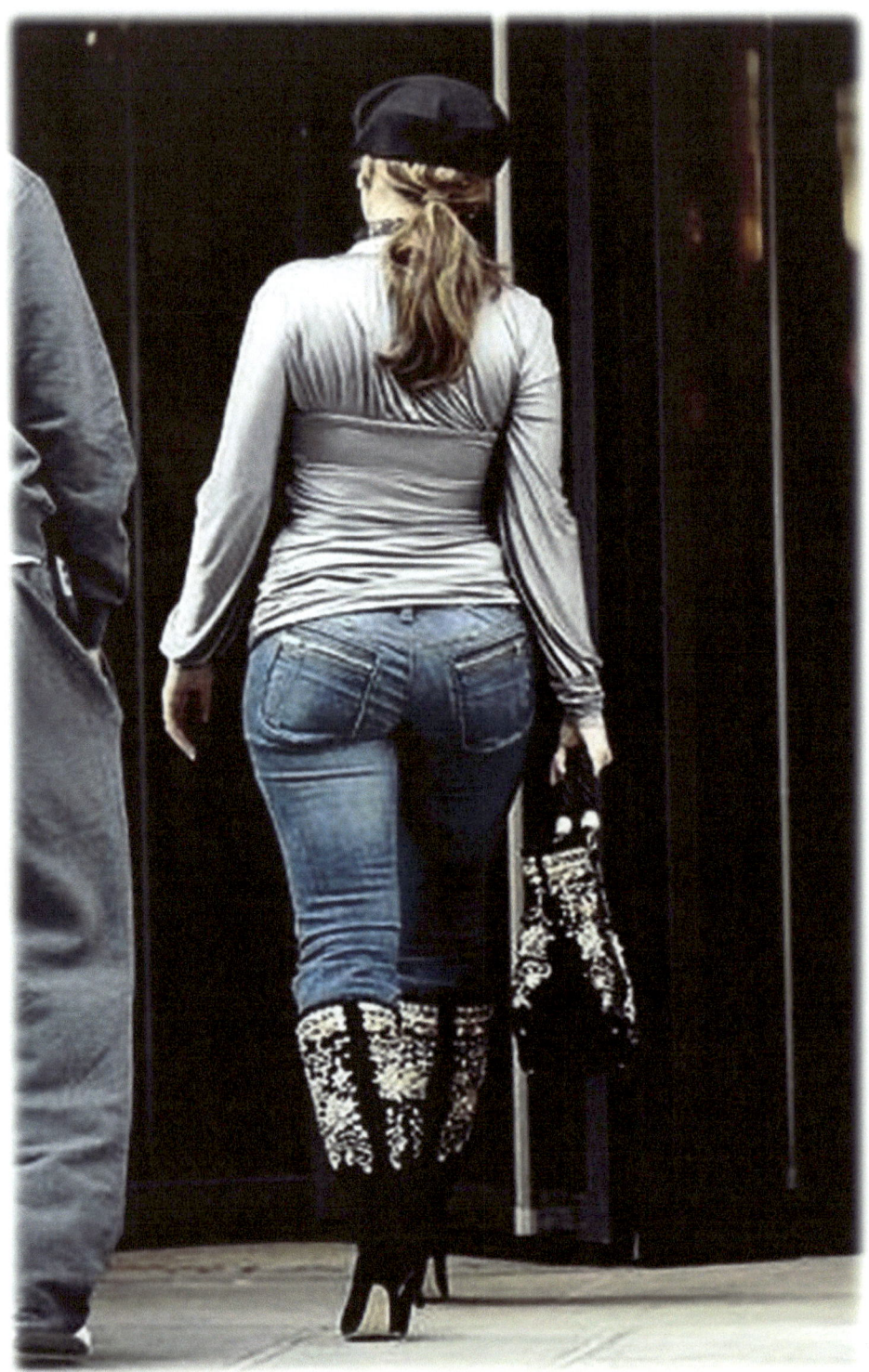

Beyoncé Photo Booklet

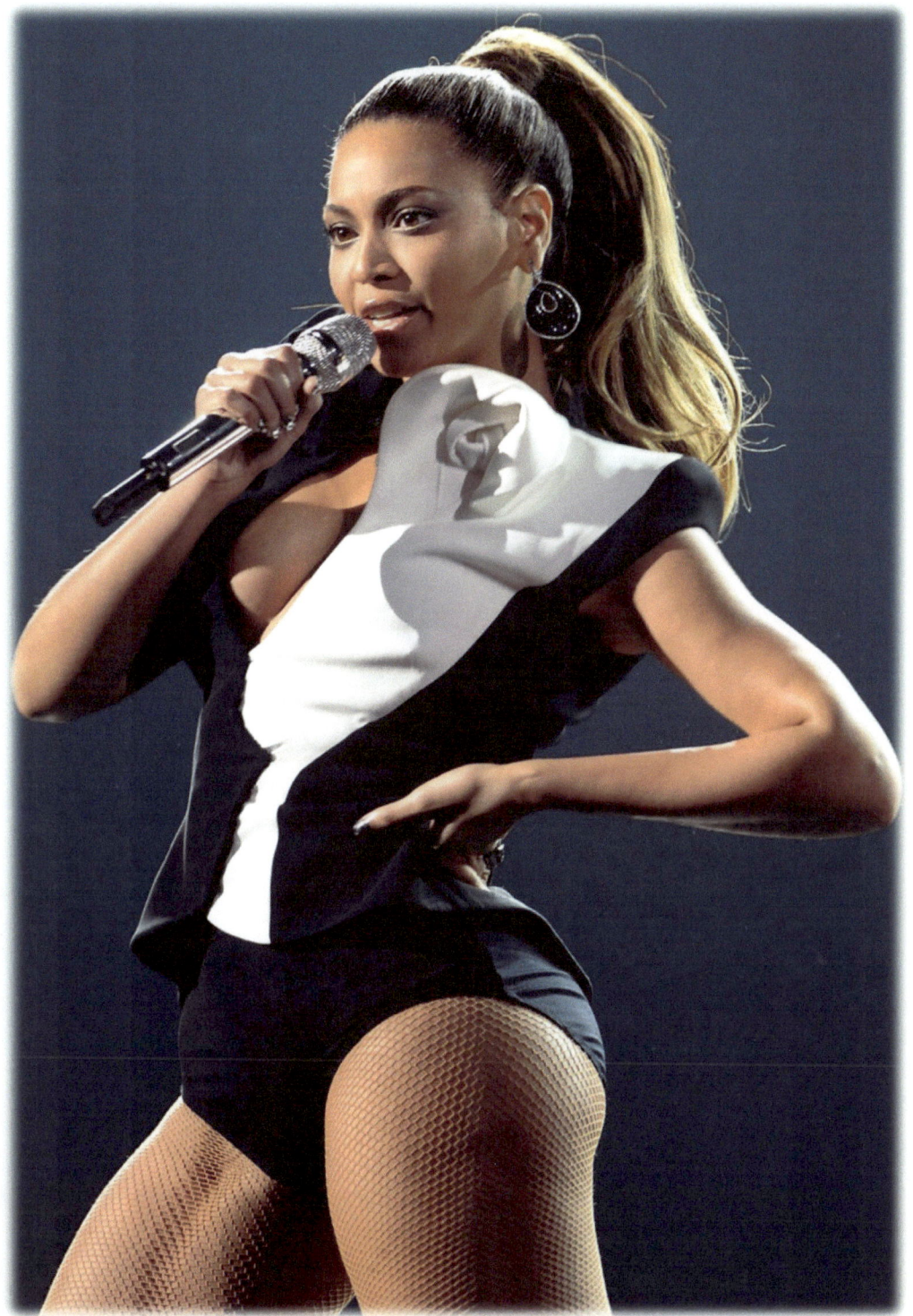

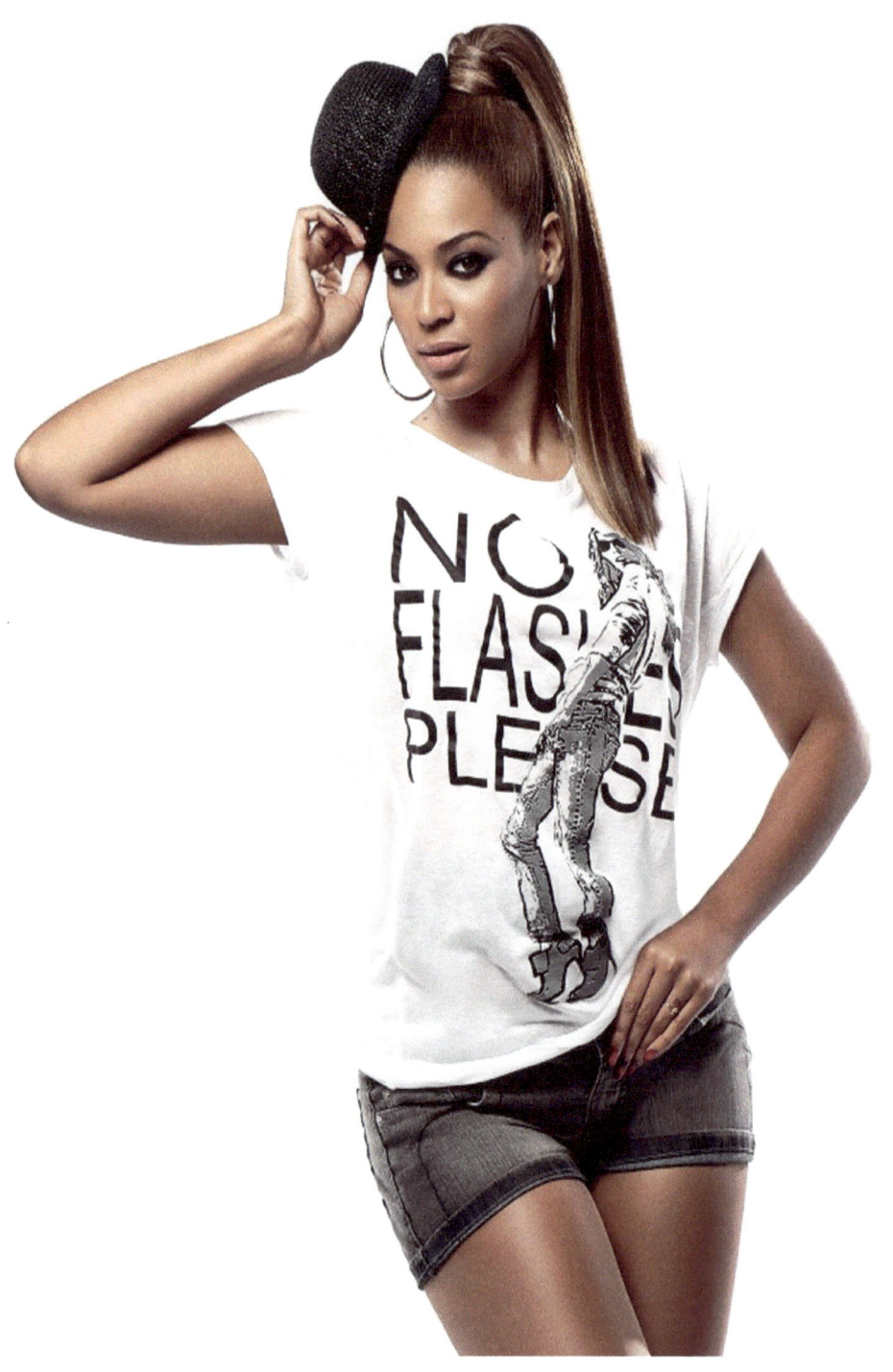

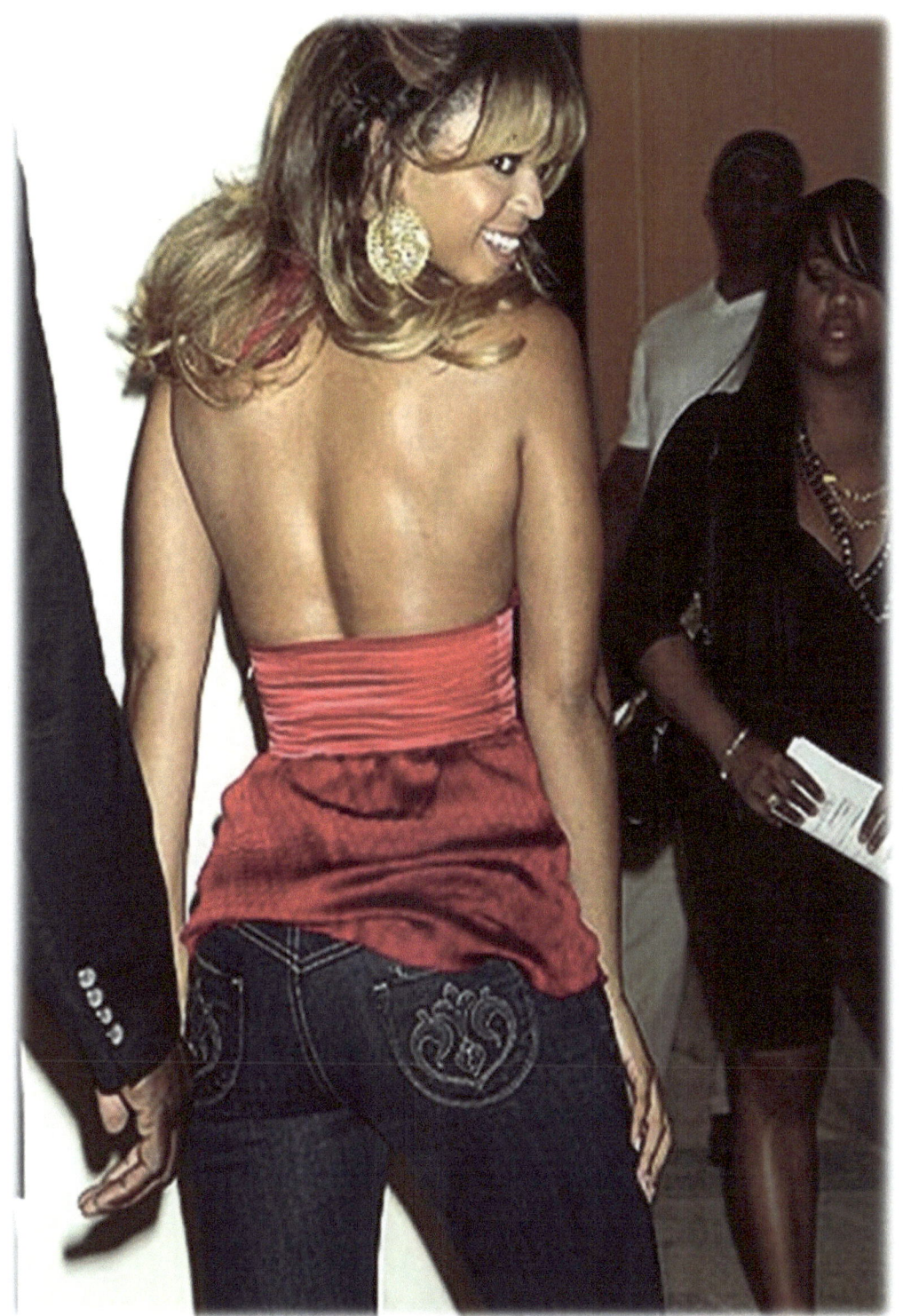

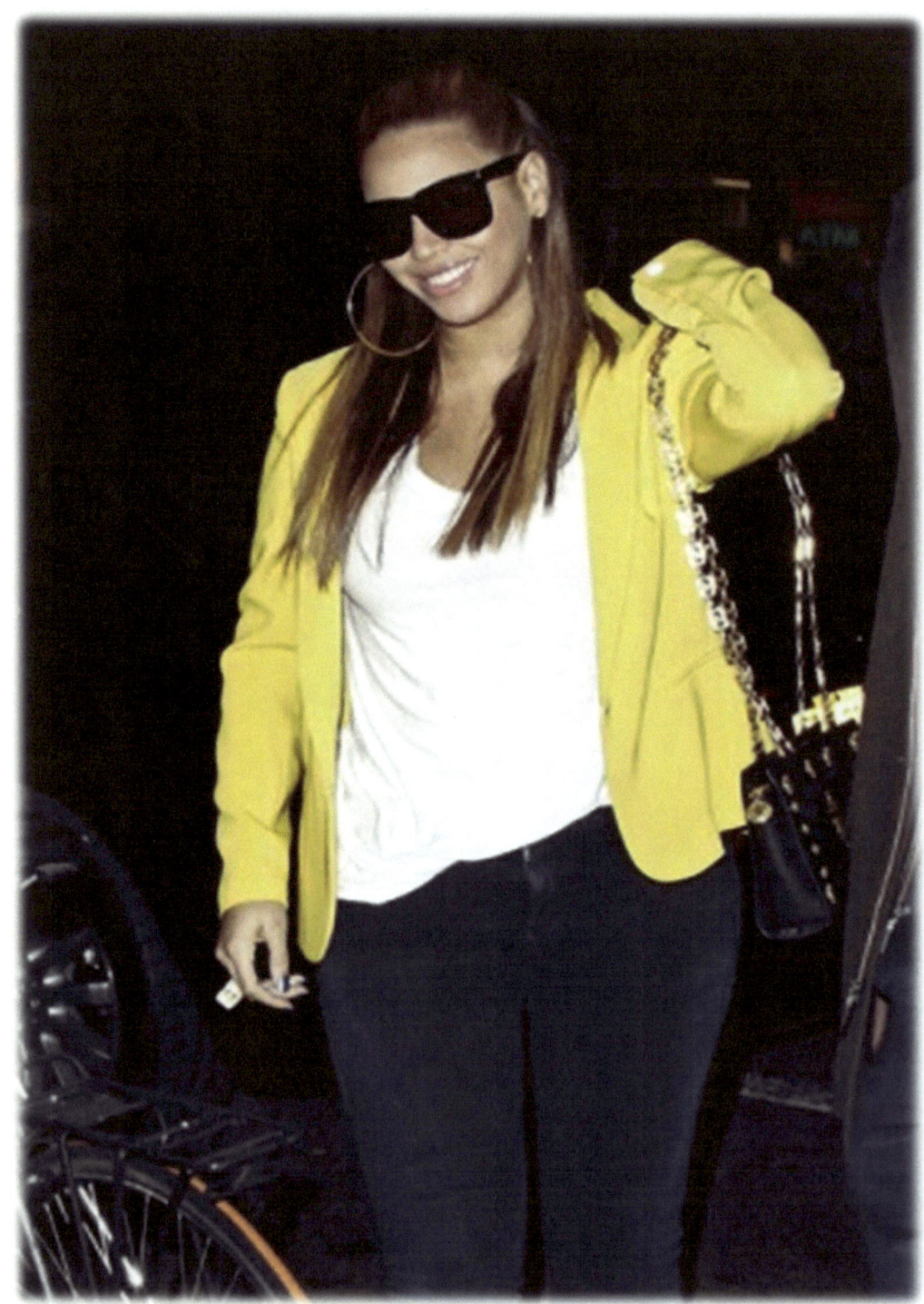

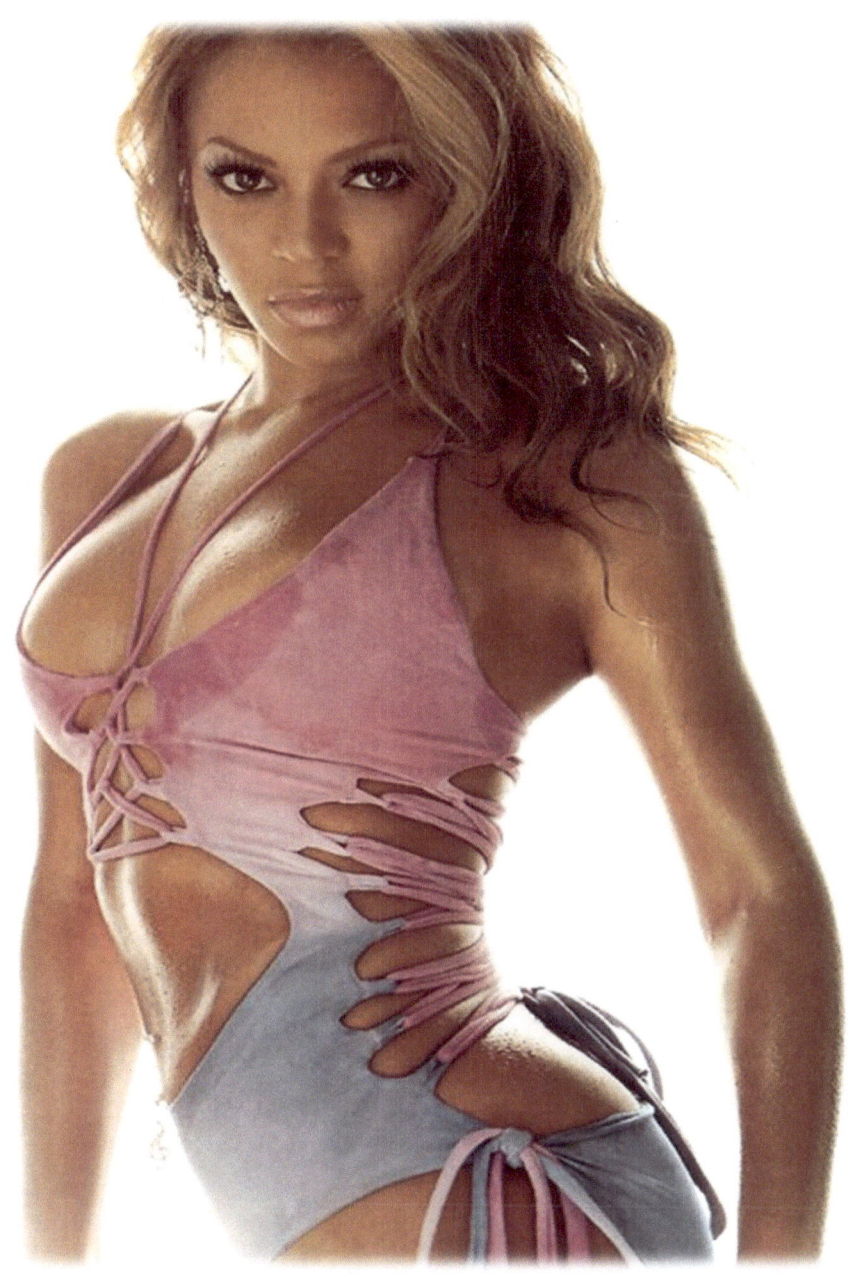

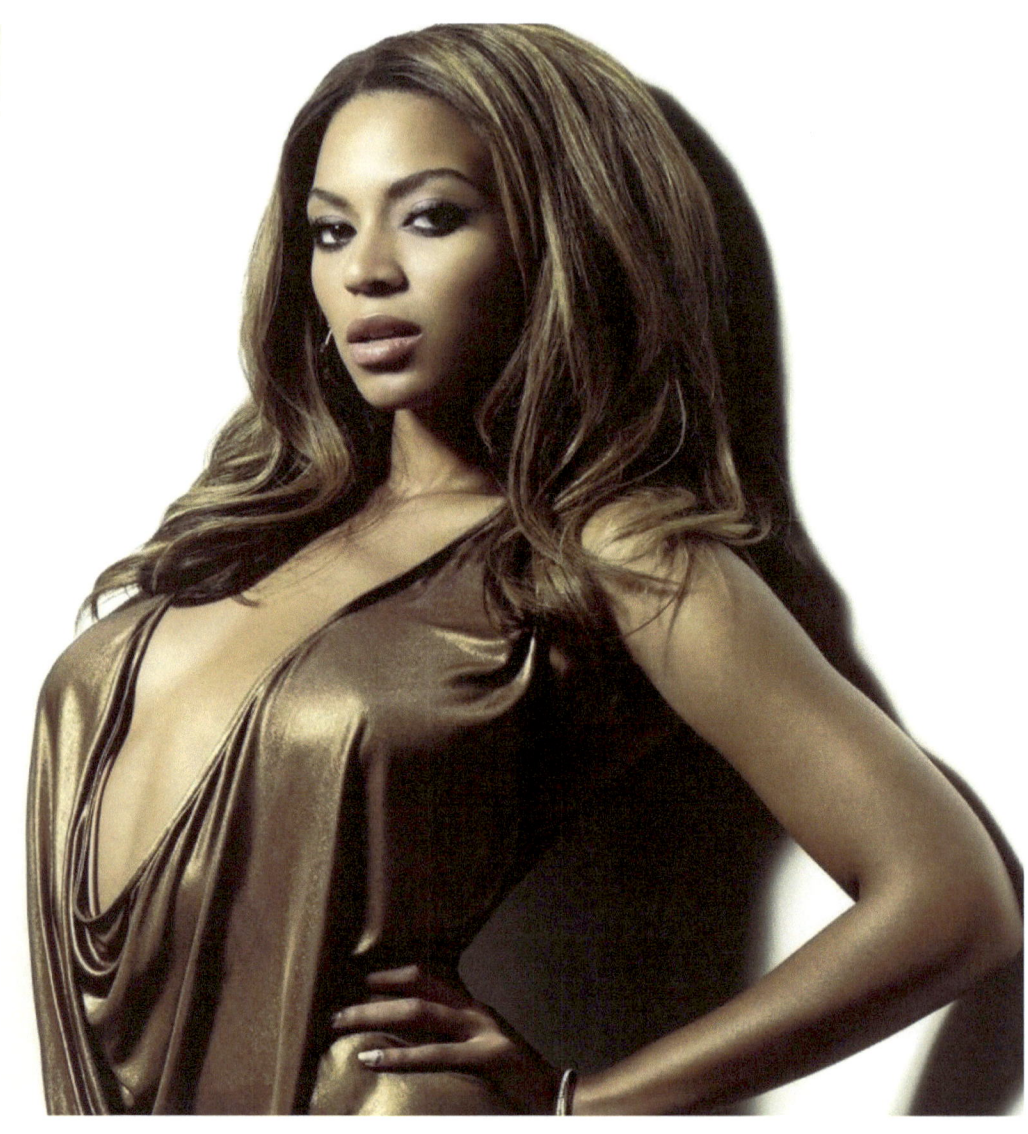

Beyoncé Photo Booklet

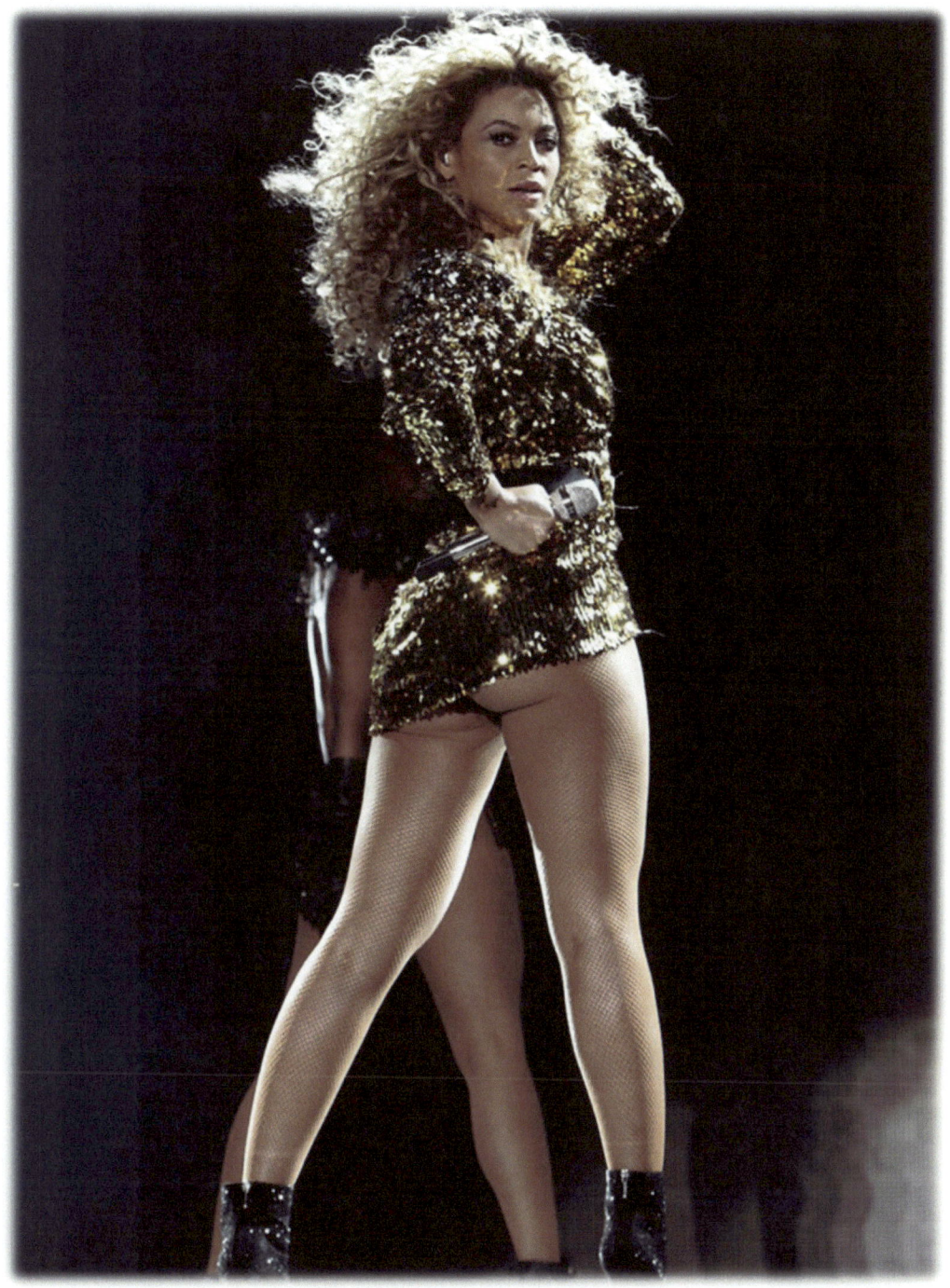

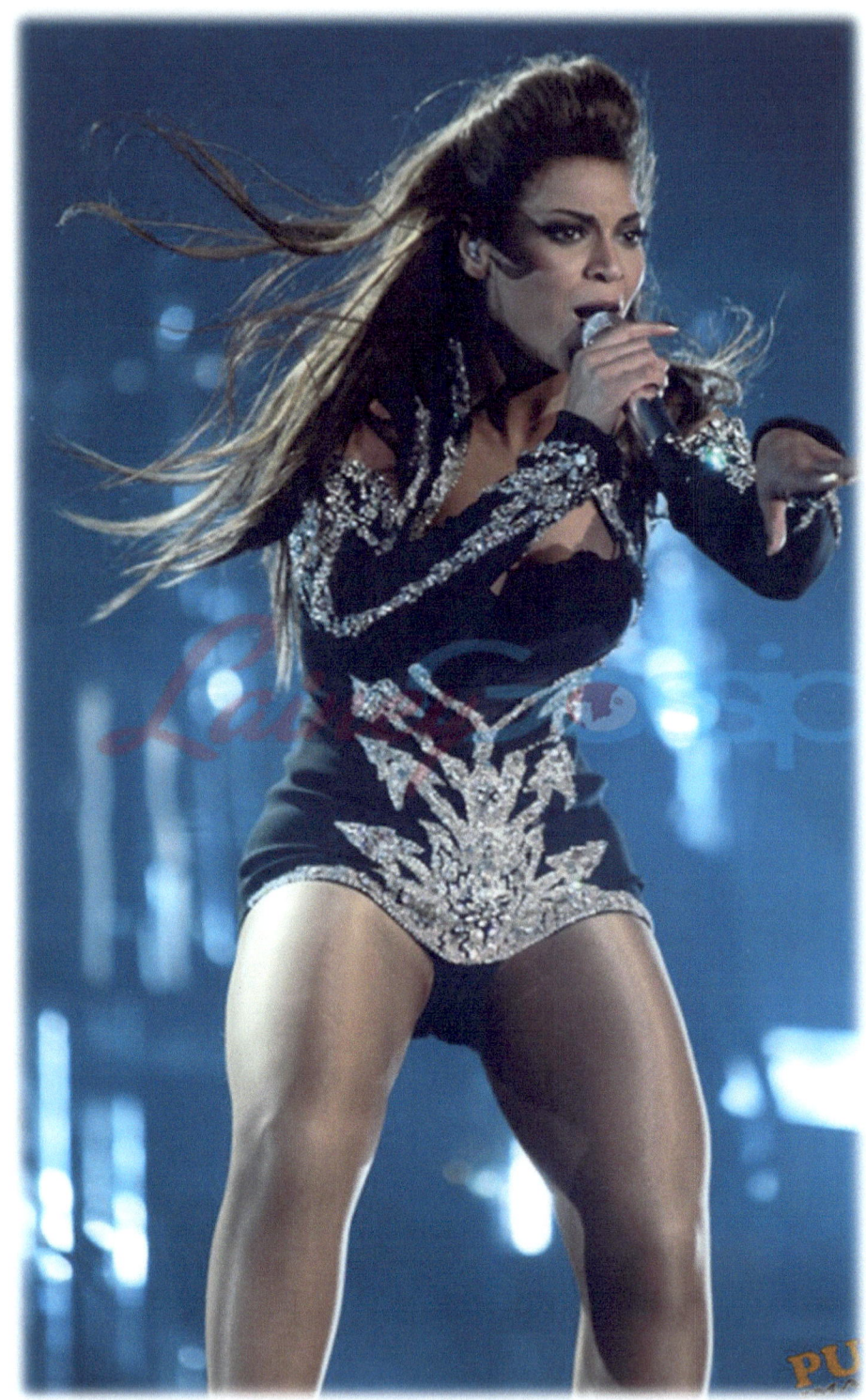

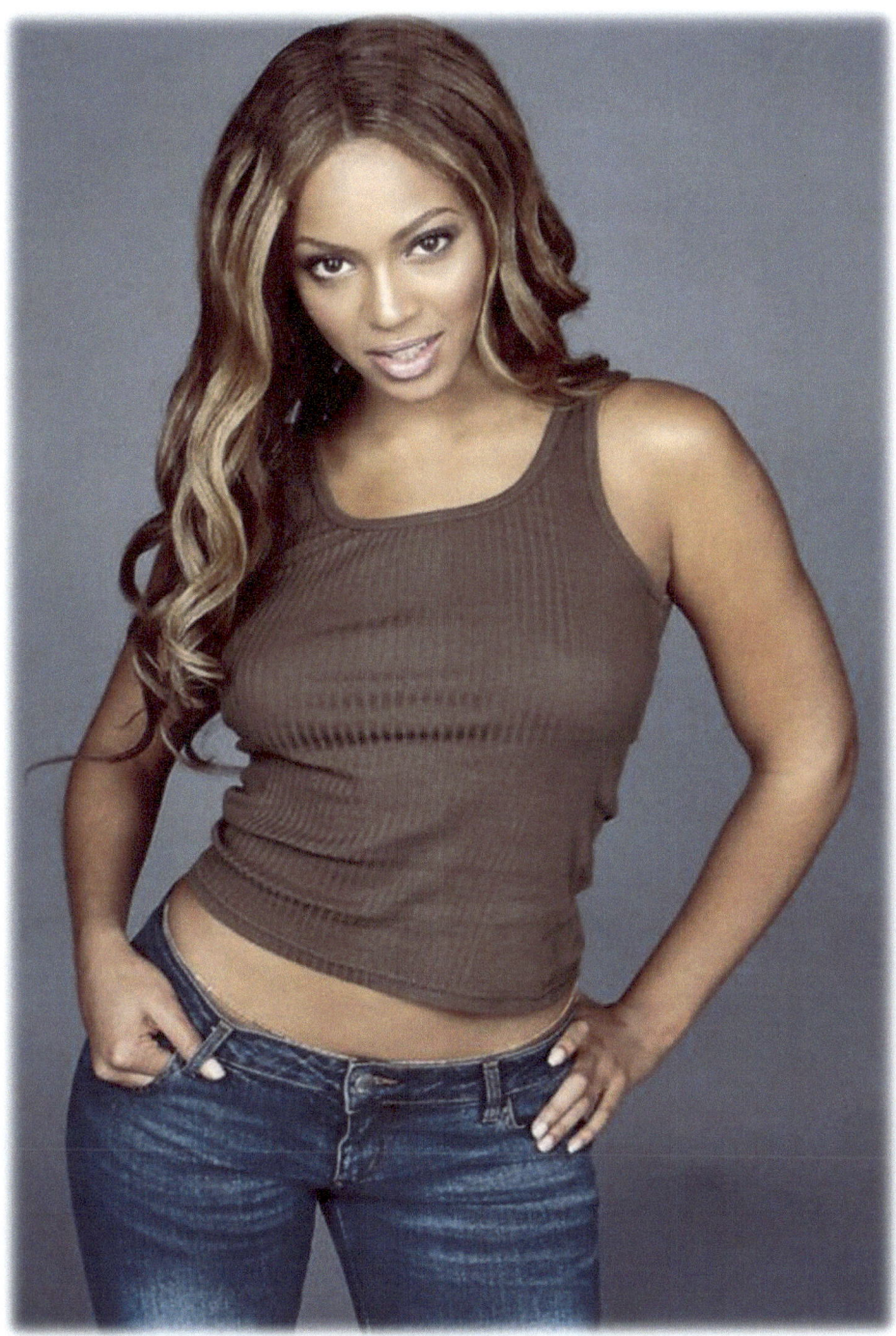

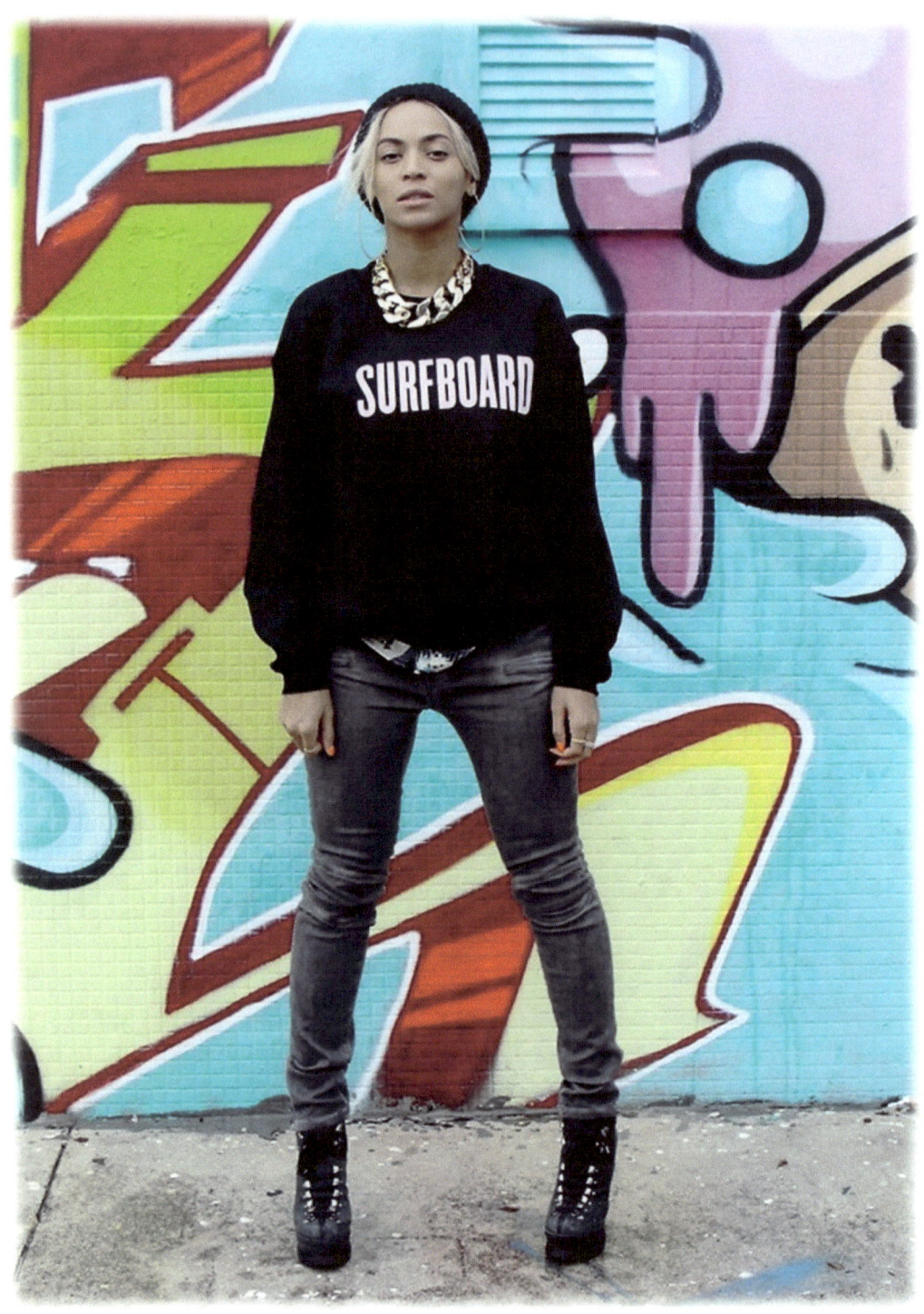

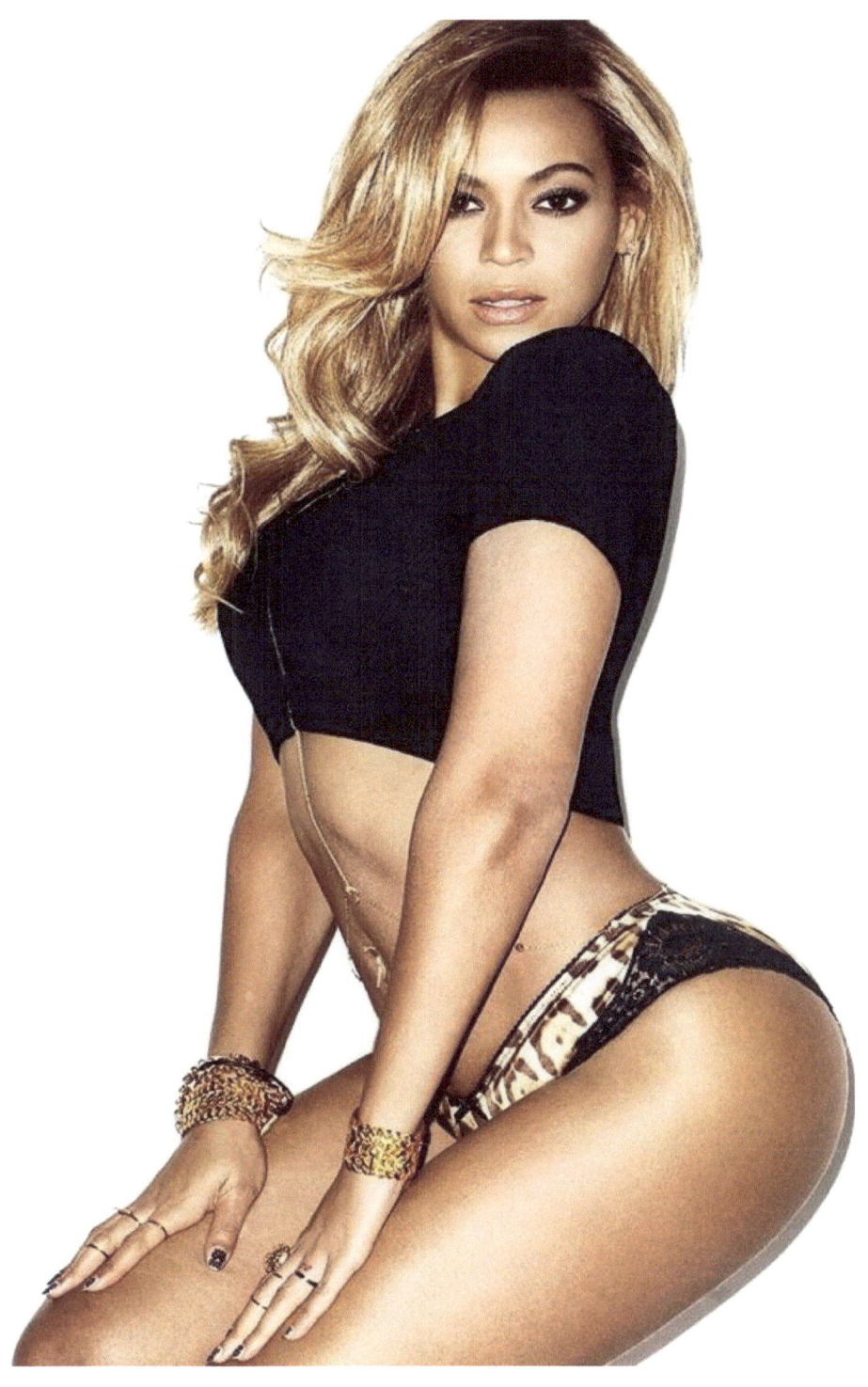

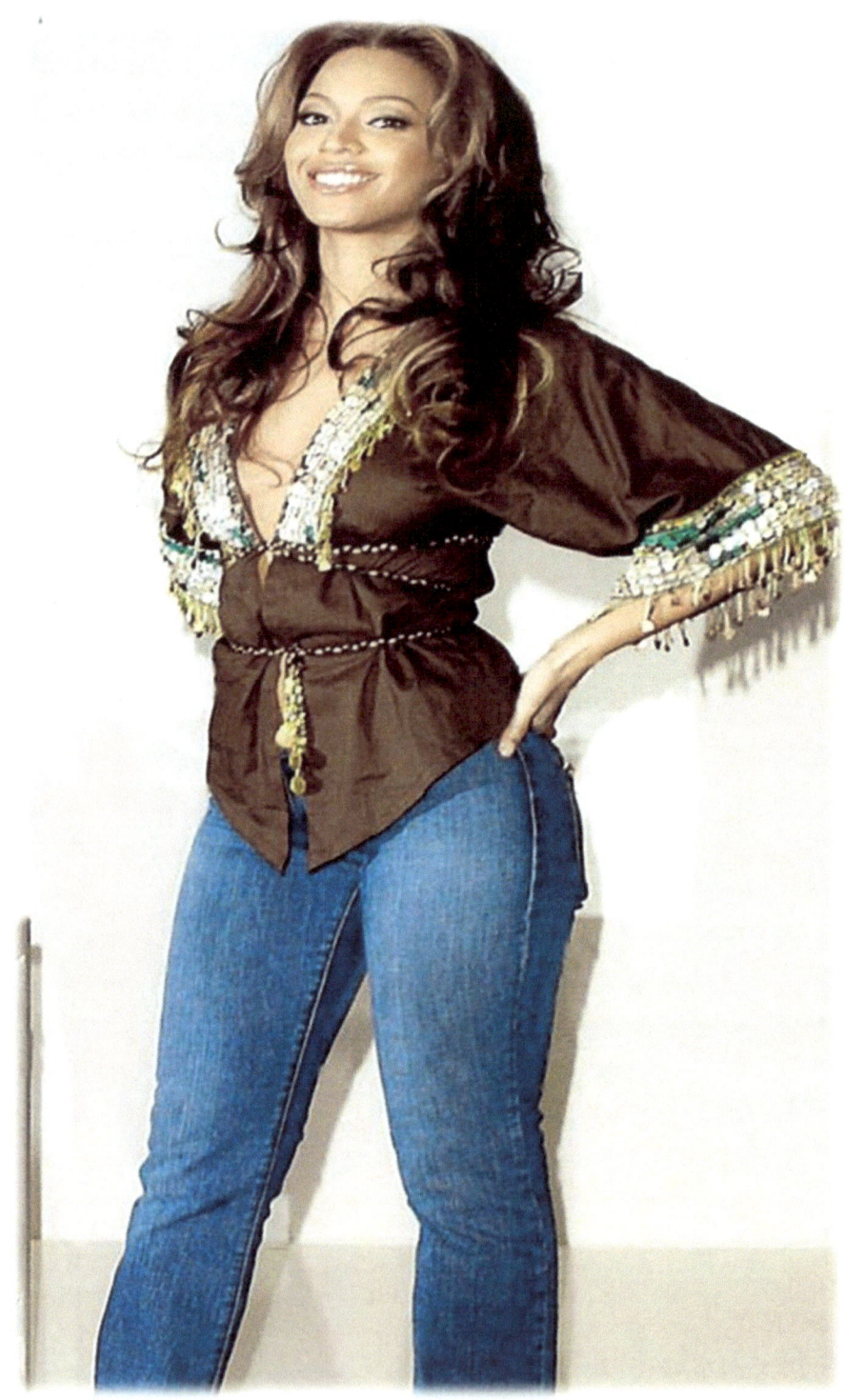

Beyoncé Photo Booklet

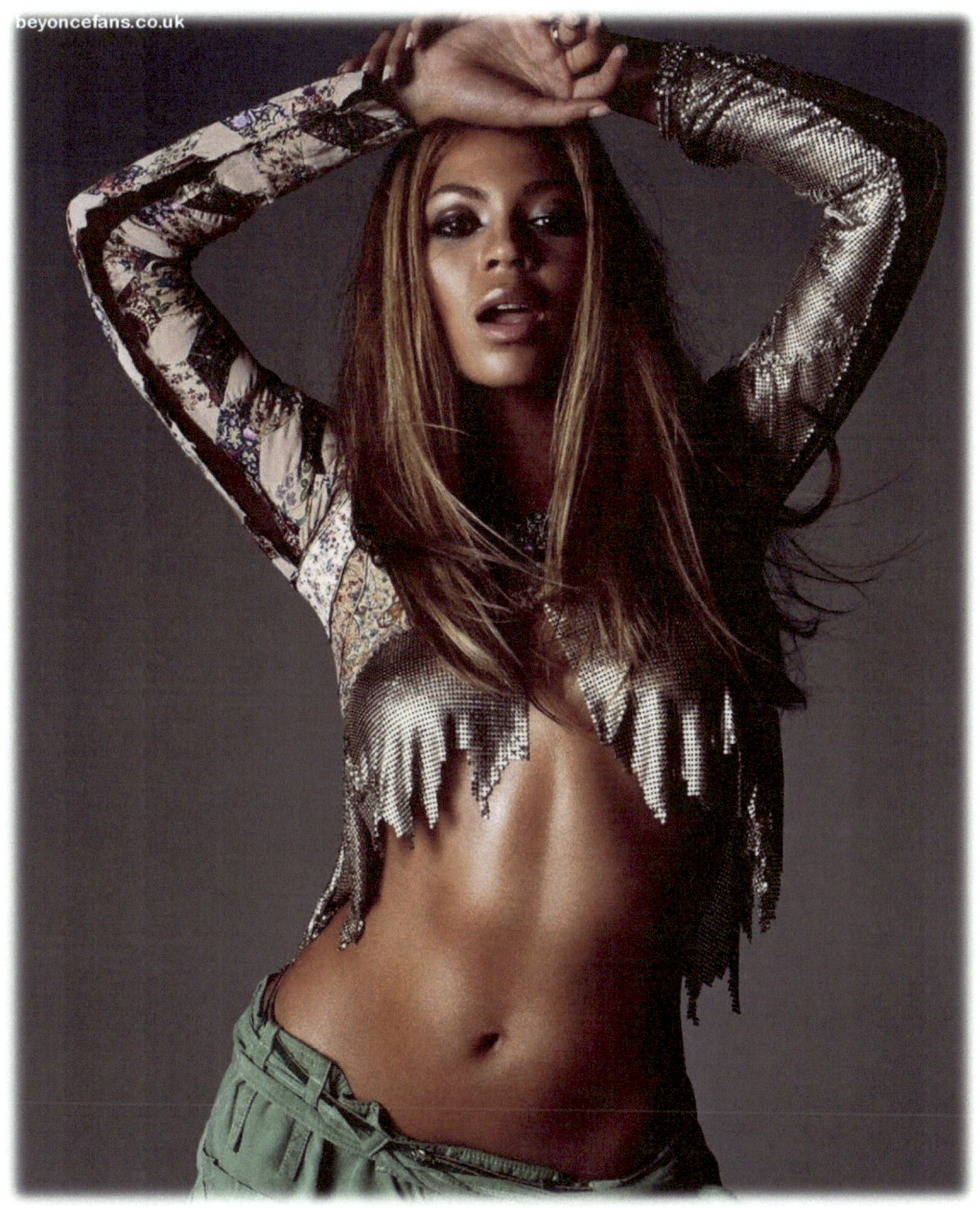

beyoncefans.co.uk

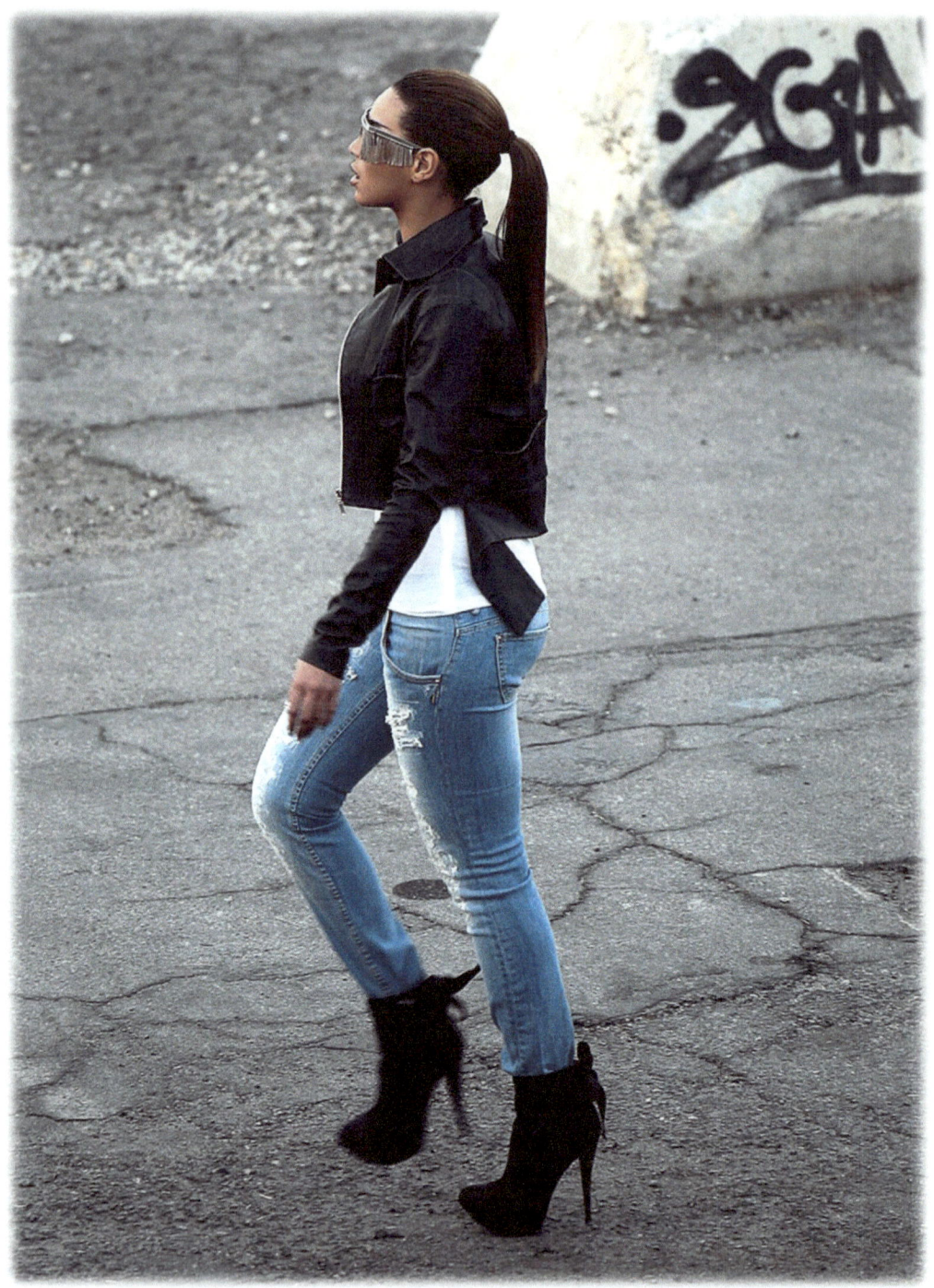

Beyoncé Photo Booklet

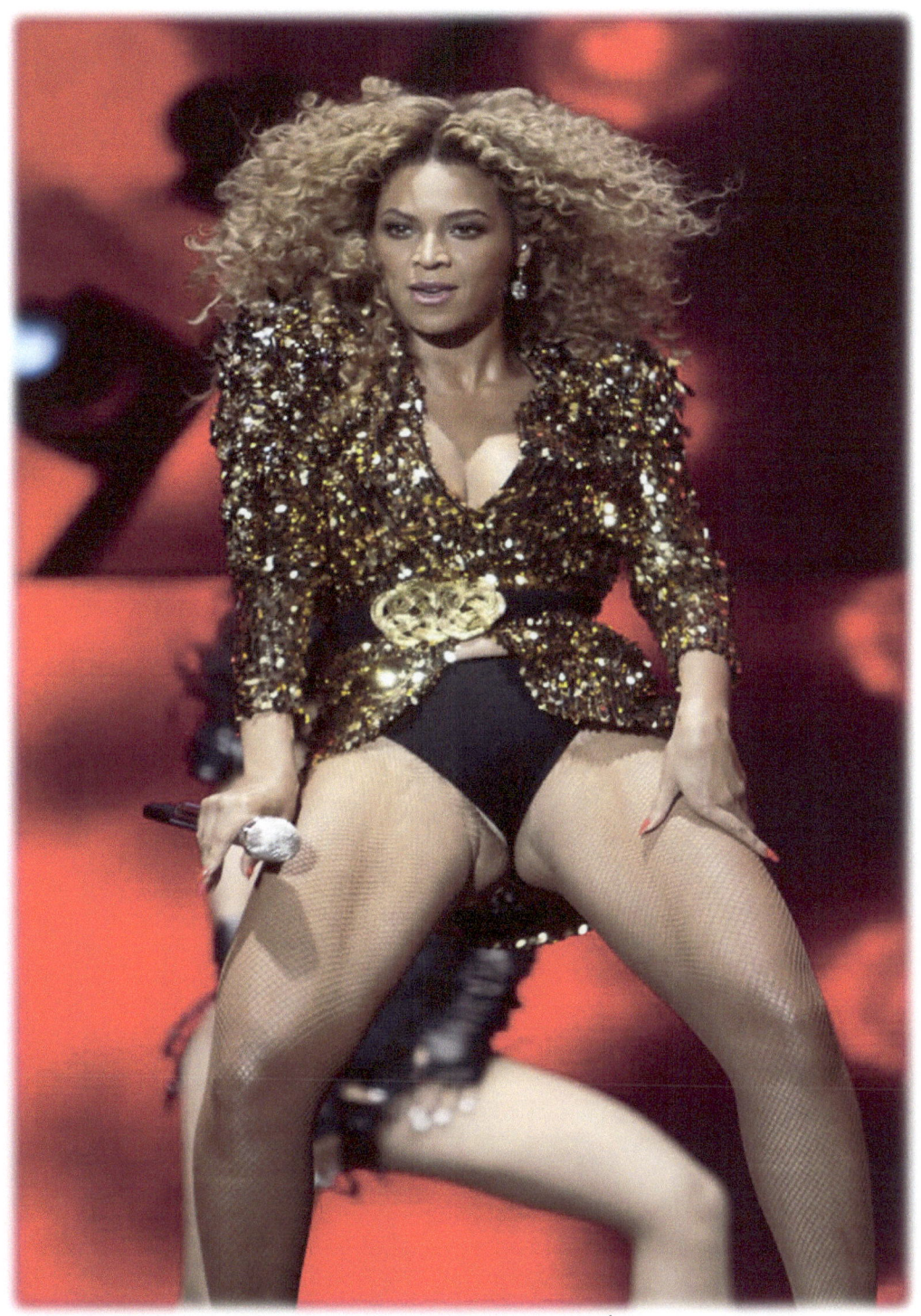

Beyoncé Photo Booklet

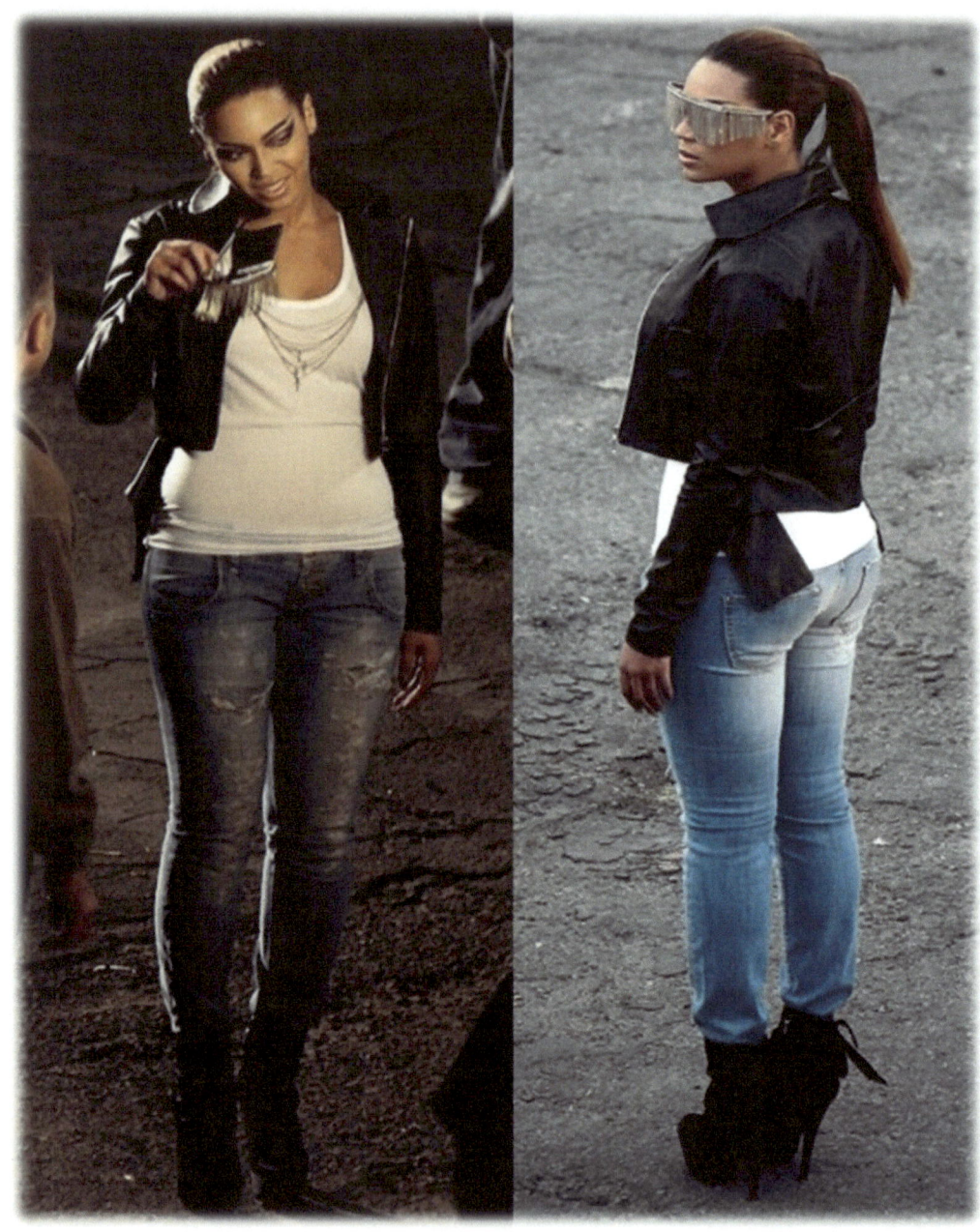

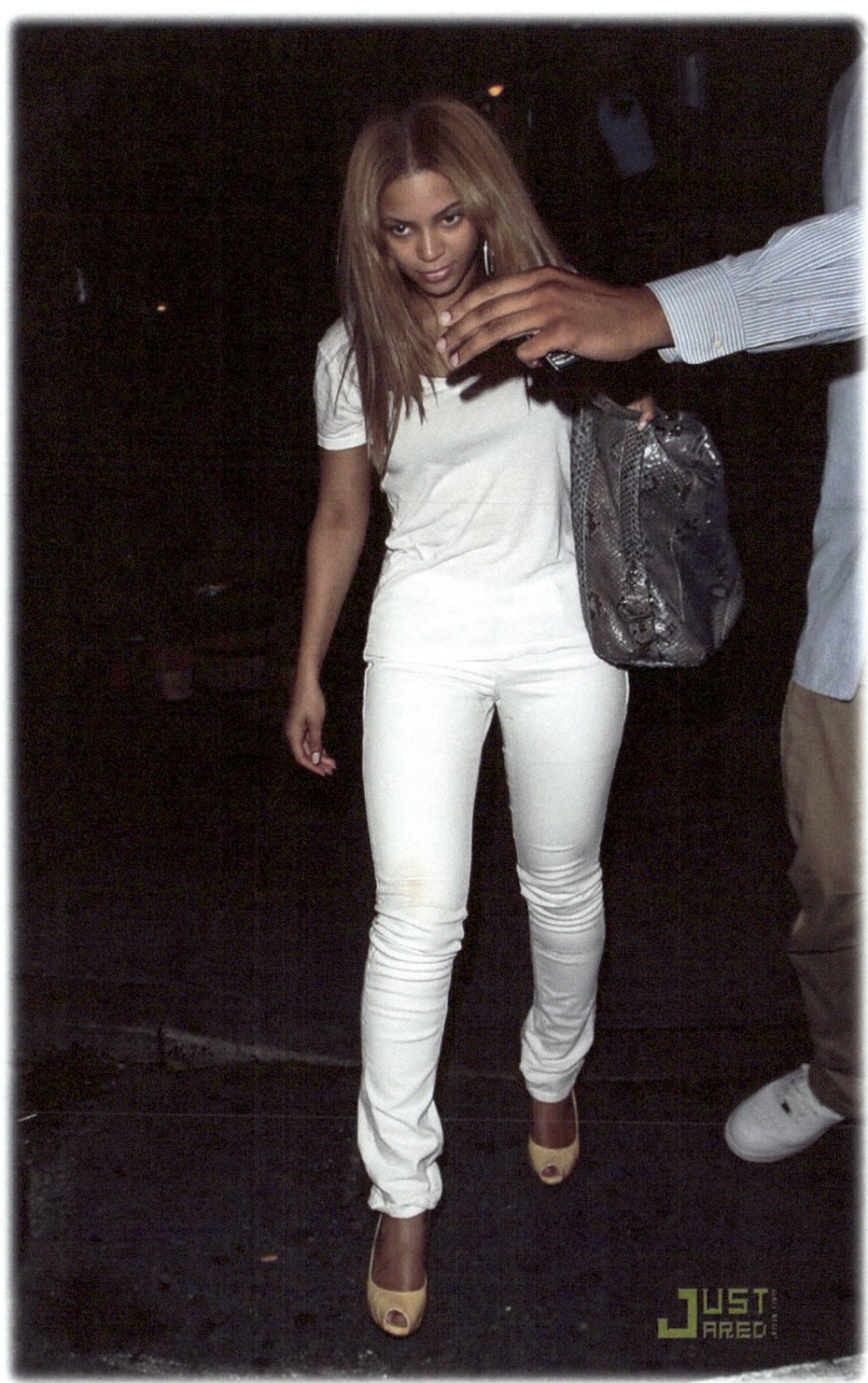

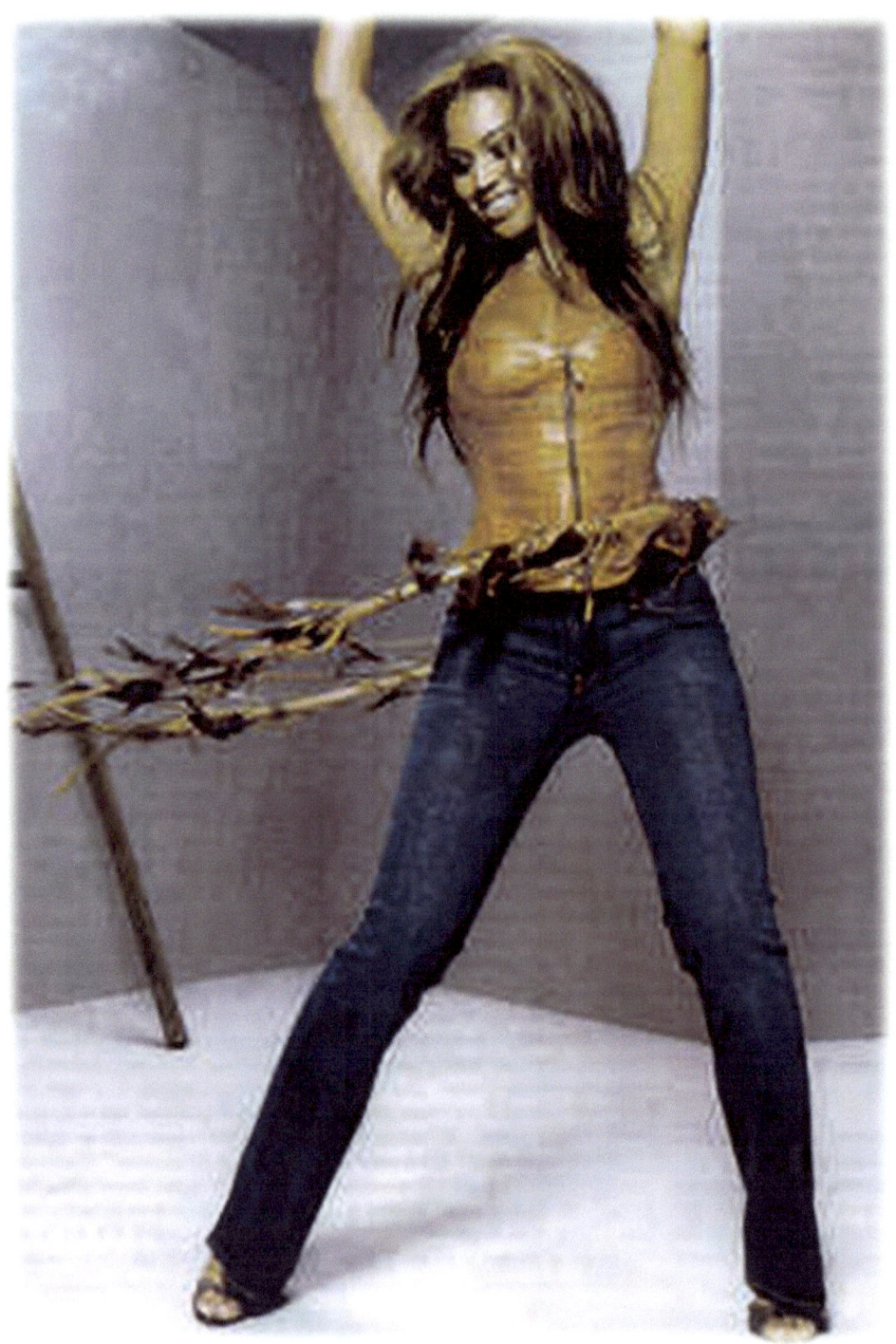

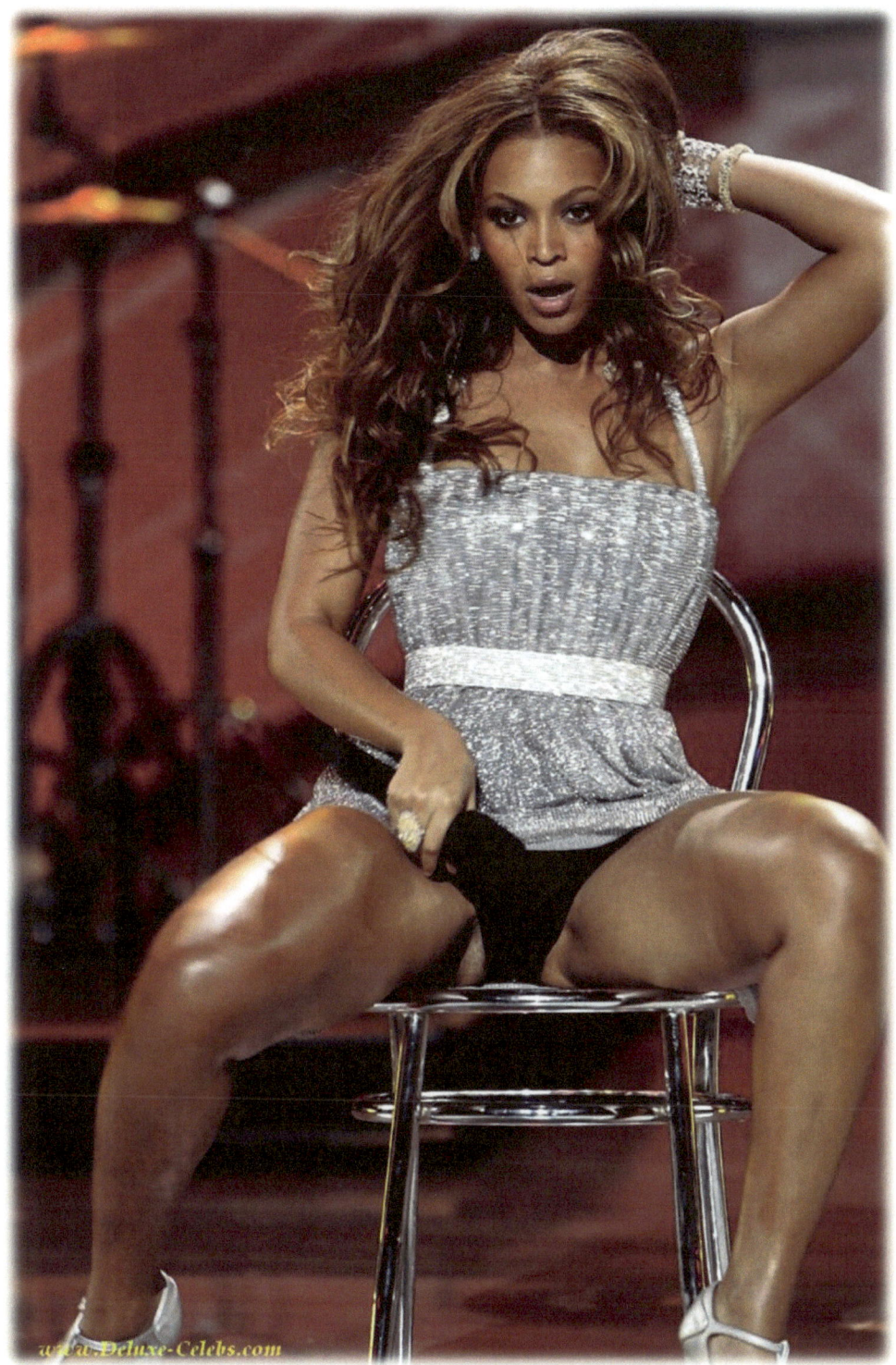

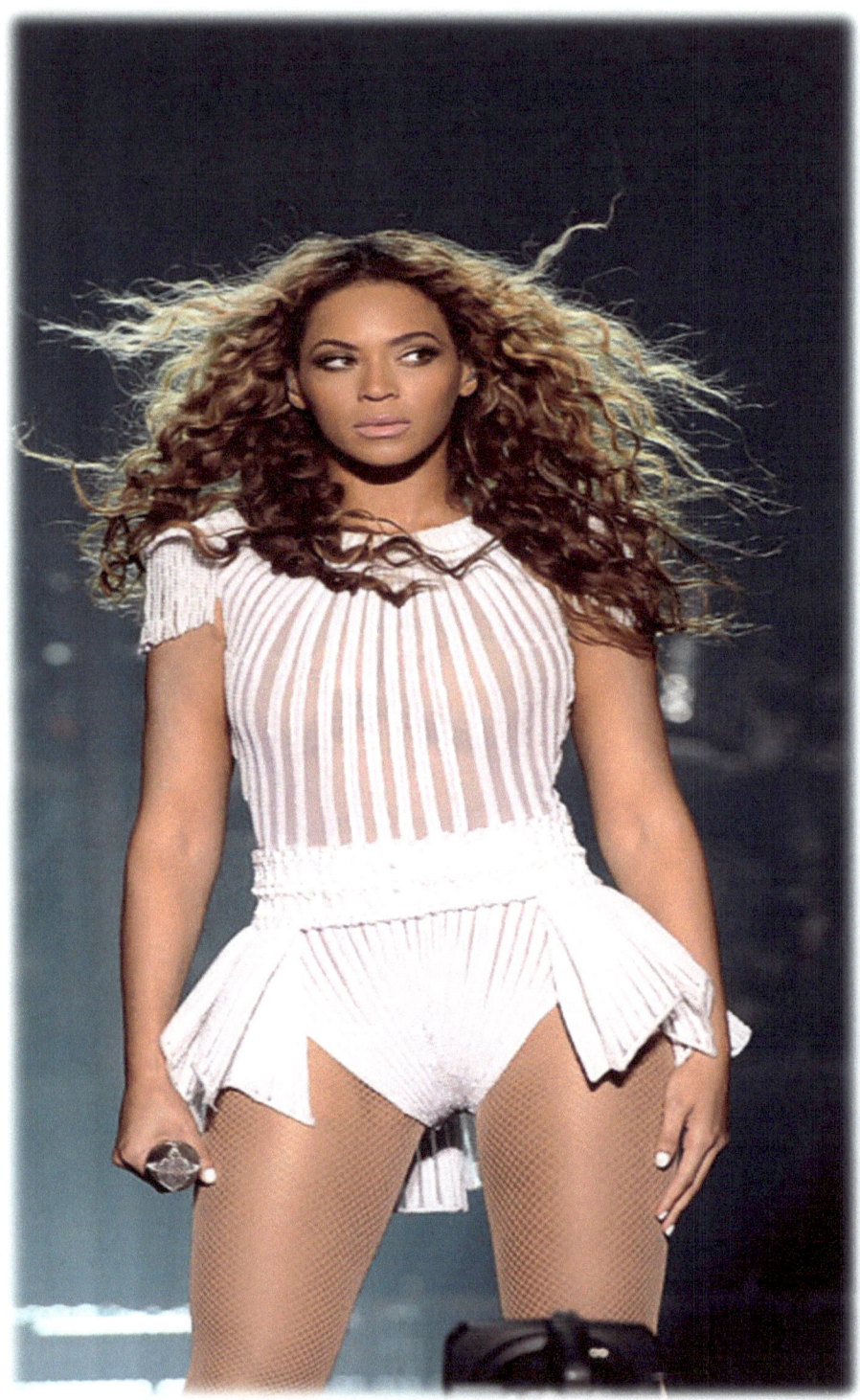

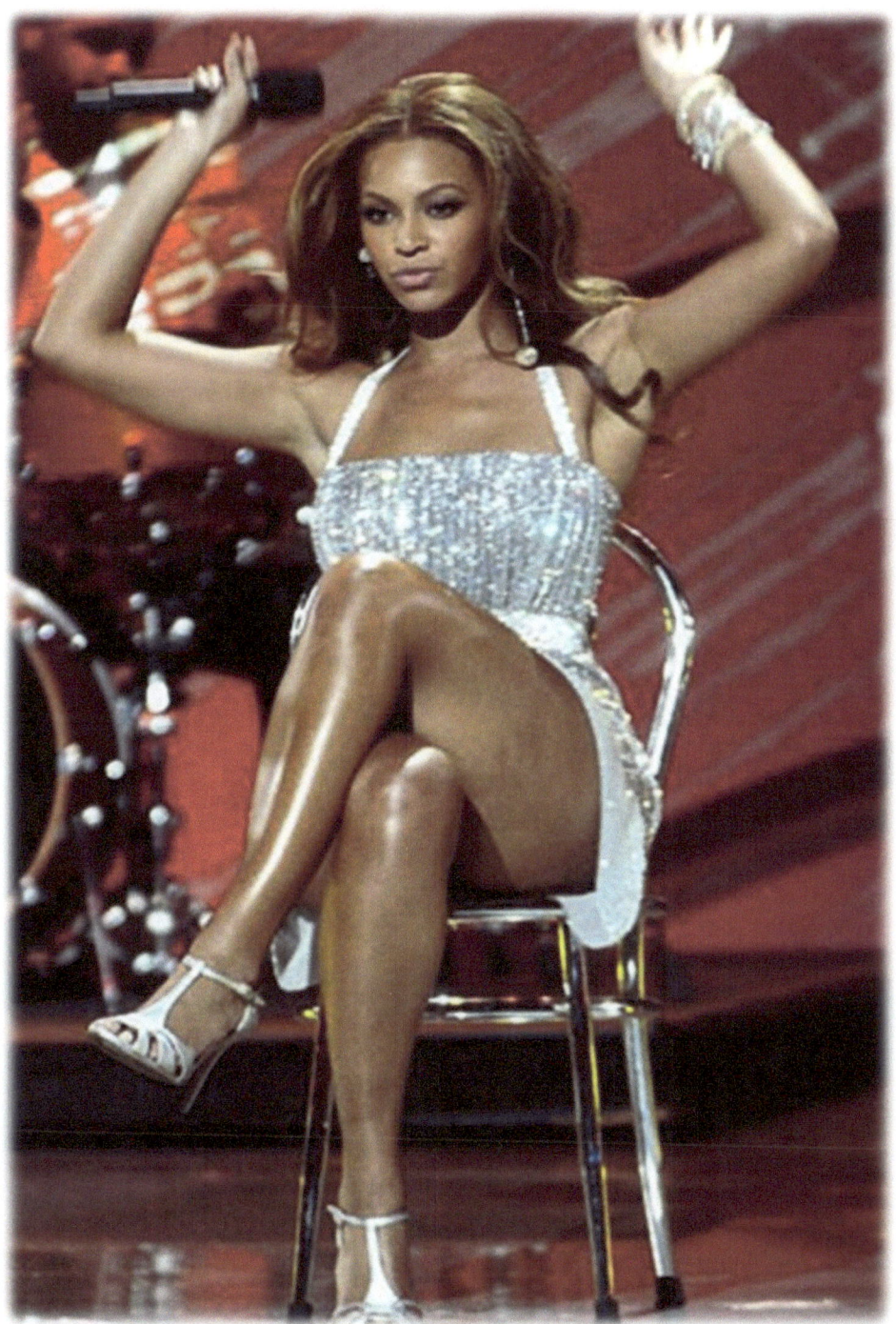

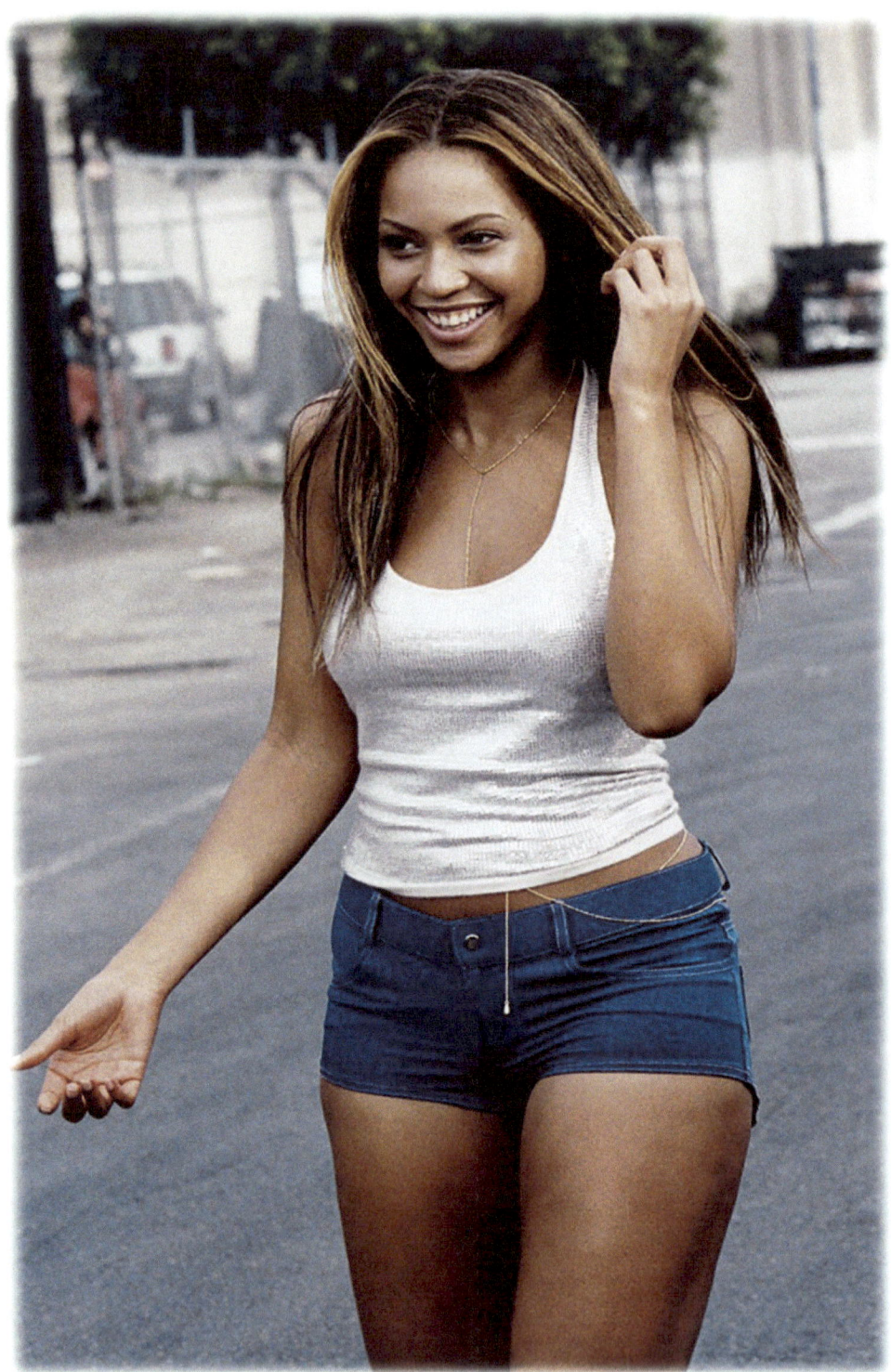

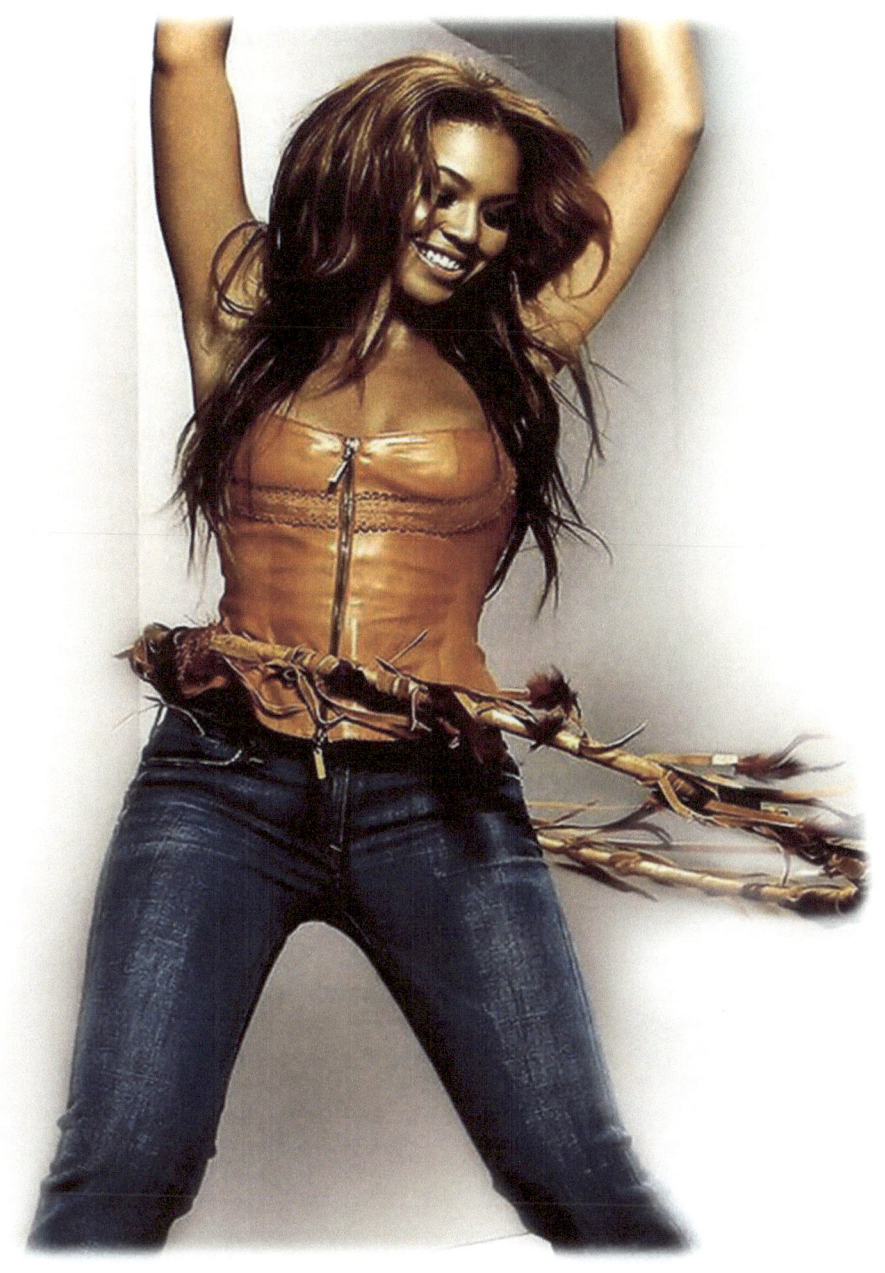

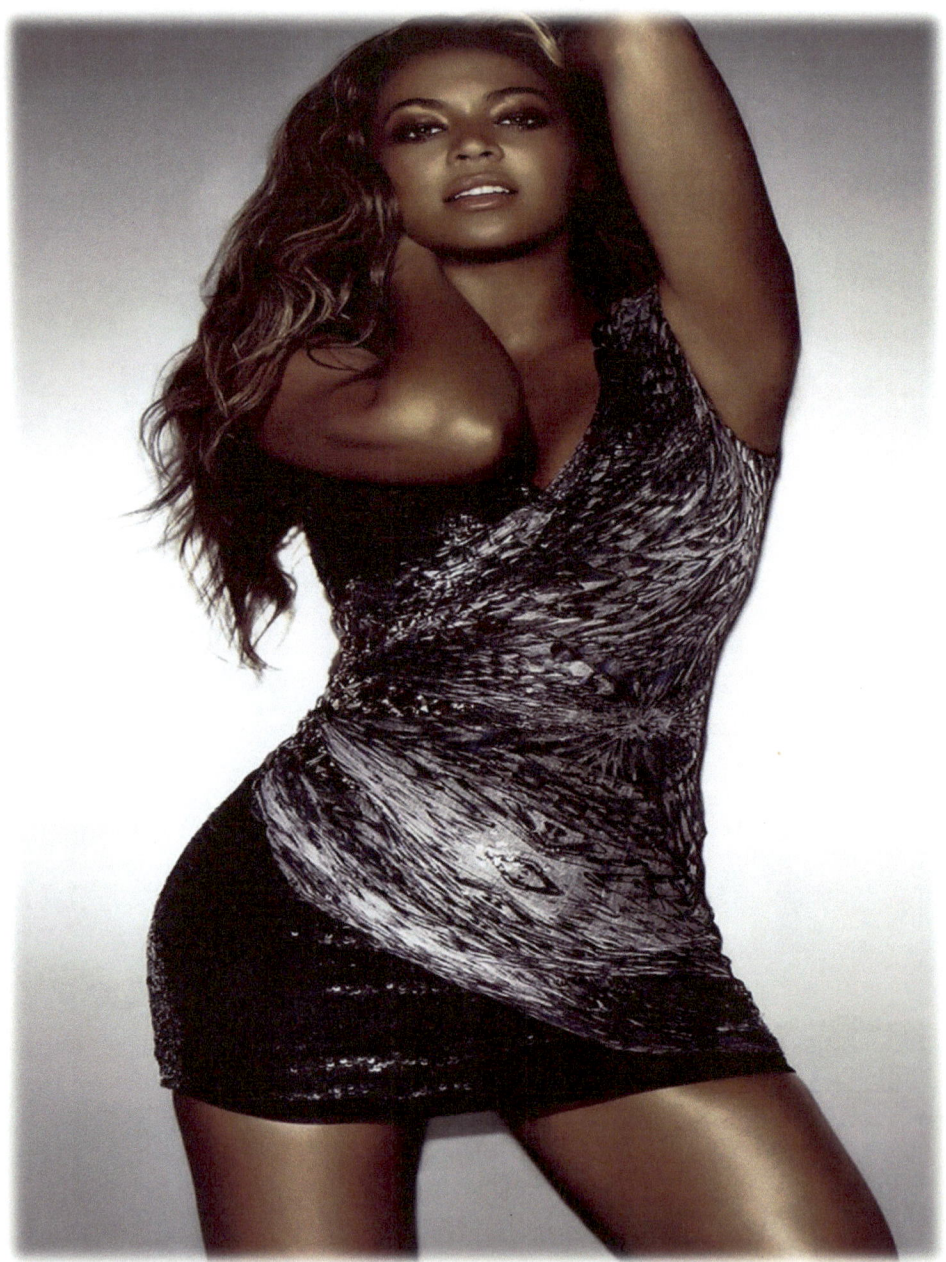

www.ingramcontent.com/pod-product-compliance
Lightning Source LLC
Chambersburg PA
CBHW041147180526
45159CB00002BB/749